Park Ranger Guide
to Rivers and Lakes

Park Ranger Guide to Rivers and Lakes

Arthur P. Miller, Jr. and Marjorie L. Miller

Illustrations by Michelle LaGory

PARK
RANGER
GUIDES

STACKPOLE BOOKS

Published by
STACKPOLE BOOKS
Cameron and Kelker Streets
P.O. Box 1831
Harrisburg, PA 17105

Printed in the United States of America

FIRST EDITION

Cover photo © Larry Lefever/Grant Heilman Photography, Inc.

Interior photos by Arthur P. Miller, Jr.

Cover design by Tracy Patterson

Interior design by Marcia Dobbs

Typesetting and page composition by Art Unlimited

Library of Congress Cataloging in Publication Data

Miller, Arthur P., Jr.
  Park ranger guide to rivers and lakes / Arthur P. Miller Jr., Marjorie L. Miller—
1st. ed.
    p. cm.
  Includes index.
  ISBN 0-8117-3038-7
  1. Stream fauna—United States—Identification. 2. Stream plants—United
States—Identification. 3. Lake fauna—United States—Identification. 4. Lake
flora—United States—Identification. 5. Rivers—United States—Guide books. 6.
Lakes—United States—Guide books. 7. Stream ecology—United States. 8. Lake
ecology—United States. I. Miller, Marjorie L. (Marjorie Lyman) II. Title
QL155.M55 1991   90-10291
574.973—dc20   CIP

To Marjorie L. Lyman

*a mother whose love of all living things
and excitement about this guide series
gave us a reader whose enthusiasm
motivated our field work and, through it,
the contents of these pages.*

Contents

CHAPTER

1

Introduction to Rivers and Lakes

"The perpendicular and even juting [sic] rocks so closely hemmed in the river that there was no possibility of passing along the shore," wrote explorer Meriwether Lewis in his expedition diary about the treacherous Salmon River.

The year was 1804 and Lewis, his coleader William Clark, and their intrepid expedition had just overcome hunger, cold, and exhaustion to cross the Continental Divide of the Rocky Mountains and reach the westward-flowing rivers that would guide them to their destination—the Pacific Ocean.

"The bed of the river was obstructed by sharp-pointed rocks and the rapidity of the stream such that the whole surface of the river was beat into perfect foam," Lewis wrote, now convinced that he and his band of adventurers had to find a less turbulent stream to continue their journey. Turning to the Clearwater River, which led into the Snake and finally into the Columbia River, they completed their epic exploration of the continent three months later, a crossing accomplished primarily by boat on the country's rivers.

Since the days of Lewis and Clark many Americans have come to know the network of rivers, streams, and lakes that spreads across the United States. The Salmon River's foaming rapids, which presented such a challenge to Lewis and Clark, now challenge a new breed of adventurers: whitewater rafters, canoeists, kayakers, and fishermen.

Rivers and lakes provide a circulation system for our nation similar to the veins and arteries of the human body. More than 3.5 million miles of waterways flow through every section of the country and affect the lives of its citizens in countless ways. Almost everyone has a river or a lake near his home.

As they populated the land the early settlers and their descendants accepted this watery network as a natural resource. Sailing their ships across the Atlantic Ocean, they navigated as far as they could up the rivers to establish towns and cities. Then they used the rivers as watery highways to press on into the interior. They found that the rivers also came in handy when defining the boundaries of developing political jurisdictions.

Homesteaders dipped water from the nearest creek or stream to nourish their families and carried it to the fields to water their animals and crops. Farmers took the corn and wheat they grew to the nearest mill where river-powered waterwheels ground it into meal or flour.

Waterpower, generated by rivers and streams, also turned the wheels of the first factories. The influx of people to run these factories gave birth to towns and cities along the riverbanks. Inventors, demonstrating that waterpower could produce electricity as well as grind corn, led the way toward industrialization. Years later, when hydroelectric power proved insufficient, river water found another use—cooling electric generators that ran on coal, oil, or nuclear fuel.

Rivers and large lakes also provided the means to take manufactured products and farm produce to market. Rafts, boats, and barges carried the raw materials to the manufacturing plant and the finished products to the market—an inexpensive transportation link between the producer and the consumer.

But these busy entrepreneurs and farmers not only used the inland waterways to develop and feed a growing nation, they also abused them. They cut too many trees from the riverbanks, stripping the rivers of their protective margin of vegetation and leaving them vulnerable to erosion. They dug into the hillsides for coal but allowed rainfall that leached acid from their spoil piles to run into the waterways. They plowed and fertilized their fields but allowed the runoff to carry soil and chemicals into rivers and lakes. They ran pipes from their factories and municipal sewage treatment plants to the closest river or lake to dump their refuse.

About thirty years ago many Americans realized what collective harm they had done to their rivers and lakes. Now mothers had to warn their children not to swim in the rivers. Fishermen walked home dejectedly with only a few fish on their string—and those were inedible. Canoeists and boaters pored for hours over maps to find a stream or lake clear enough for a day's cruise or a camping trip.

Gradually, however, the workings of a democratic form of government converted the environmental concerns of a large number of people into state and federal regulations designed to preserve the rivers and lakes that remained unspoiled and to clean up those that had become polluted.

Wisconsin enacted the first state wild and scenic river act in 1965. Maine in 1966 designated the Allagash River, a real challenge for canoeists, as a "wilderness waterway." In 1968 Congress followed with the Wild and Scenic Rivers Act, which authorized the federal government to preserve selected inland waters as wild rivers that flow through wilderness areas, or as scenic or recreational rivers. Today, segments of 120 rivers across the country totaling 9,281 miles are protected in the National Wild and Scenic River System. To be considered, a river must possess "outstandingly remarkable scenic, recreational, geologic, fish and wildlife, historic, cultural, or similar values." Rivers may be designated in one of three categories, based on their natural qualities and on how free they are from the intrusions of man:

1. *Wild river.* One whose waters are unpolluted and un-dammed and that people can reach only by foot or by horseback. Its watershed and shoreline must be essentially primitive.

2. *Scenic river.* One with scenic attributes that remains undammed, has only limited development along its shorelines, but which can be reached by road at places.

3. *Recreational river.* A river, either free-flowing or impound-ed to form a lake, that offers potential for a variety of water sports and activities. A recreational river is readily accessible by road and may have considerable development such as cottages and concessions along its shores.

Meanwhile, thirty-two states have river conservation programs of their own that protect more than twelve thousand additional miles of their scenic rivers and streams.

To preserve the water quality of the nation's rivers, Congress in 1948 enacted the Federal Water Pollution Control Act, which regulates the discharge of pollutants into rivers, streams, and lakes and sets standards for clean water. These provisions were further strengthened in 1977 by the Clean Water Act, which promotes the protection of fish and wildlife and encourages cooperative conservation measures between federal and state governments.

As for lakes, a number of them are preserved in their natural state within the boundaries of national parks, national wildlife refuges, national forests, and state parks. The National Park Service conserves sections of lake shorelines as part of four national lakeshores. Numerous man-made lakes, or reservoirs, formed by damming the rivers, provide recreation for many people as well as water for irrigation and electric power generation.

Not many years ago Lake Erie was reported to be "dead," but thanks to cleanup programs by the United States and Canada, today is again teeming with fish. The waters of other Great Lakes have also improved due to cooperative efforts.

This book grows out of a need for a guide to some of the better places to experience a wild or scenic river or a national lakeshore, to learn something of the ecology of aquatic habitats, and to appreciate the animals, birds, and fish that live there. Who is better suited to introduce us to the natural history preserved in and around these rivers and lakes than the park and forest rangers, biologists, boatmen, guides, and interpreters who serve in the parks and refuges? It is these rangers whose job it is to protect our vast aquatic resources and to explain their significance to the public.

To gather facts for this volume, we visited scenic rivers, national rivers, national recreation areas, national parks, national lakeshores, wildlife refuges, national forests, Tennessee Valley Authority lakes, Bureau of Land Management public lands, and state parks across the country. We selected the sites described in the book to offer a cross-section of these preserved river corridors and lakes, some of the finest natural river and lake settings in America. From the examples in these preserves, grouped within five regions of the country, you will learn about the wildlife and plantlife, ecology and geology that made these rivers and lakes showcase aquatic environments. Many plants and animals, of course, exist in more than one region of the country; you will find them in these pages in the region where we observed them.

We also interviewed more than a hundred rangers, biologists, guides, interpreters, recreation specialists, researchers, park superintendents, forest managers, and refuge managers. It is their firsthand knowledge that lends authenticity to these pages.

As we canoed, rafted, boated, and swam in these rivers and lakes and hiked their shores we found these outdoors men and women to be intent on preserving the resources entrusted to them. They are also eager to share their knowledge so that each visitor will better understand and appreciate this country's heritage of inland waterways.

Ranger Assistance

Ranger guides can open up new vistas to the aquatic world around you. They demonstrate how parts of the natural world fit into a fabric and explain how plants and animals adapt to their environment. Rangers will tell you that rivers and lakes and their associated wetlands provide essential habitats for plants, animals, invertebrates, insects, and fish that live in and around them. Entire communities of plants and animals depend on these watery areas.

Wet environments, together with large amounts of nutrients, often result in an abundance of vegetation. This mass of plant material traps the sun's energy and is a driving force in a wetland. Due to their great productivity, aquatic settings are rich with diverse species, a phenomenon known as biodiversity. This variety of species that dwells in a wetland makes it a vast storehouse of genetic material.

Wetlands have other important values as well. They improve the quality of waters surrounding them by filtering out and retaining nutrients, neutralizing chemical and organic wastes, and straining out sediment. A wetland serves as a natural sponge, absorbing flood waters that overflow riverbanks or collect in isolated depressions. Trees, shrubs, and other wetland plants slow the speed of raging floods.

For many animals and plants, such as the wood duck and muskrat, the cattail and the swamp rose, wetlands are their primary habitat—the only place where they can thrive. For other animals, such as the striped bass, the endangered peregrine falcon, and the white-tailed deer, wetlands provide food, water, and cover that are important to their well being even though the wetlands may not be their primary residence. It is interesting to note that the majority of rare and endangered plants in many states depend on wetlands for their survival.

Observing wildlife from a canoe or a boat may give you a broader view than hiking along a woodland trail. Your boat, in effect, becomes a floating blind that helps you observe wildlife without disturbing it. You might find yourself in a ringside seat as a heron takes flight or a turtle slips into the water. With a little more luck you might see a raccoon come down to the water's edge to hunt for crayfish, or an otter slide down a riverbank to search for mud minnows, suckers, or sticklebacks.

It is the rangers who will give you a close-up view of these surroundings. An interpretive talk we heard one day refocused our observation powers on tiny animals like the caddisfly, the mayfly, and the stonefly—all of them larvae that live almost hidden from sight in freshwater streams.

Using other senses besides sight can help you experience a river or lake more fully. Visiting the Delaware River we were intrigued by a sensory trail. The trail winds along a tributary creek of the Delaware, through a landscape you must learn to "read" by using senses other than vision. Participants wear blindfolds and guide themselves along the one-quarter mile trail by holding onto a rope.

As you walk along, a leader will ask: "Do you hear anything here?" (You hear the gurgle of the creek.) "Do you smell something here?" (It's the aroma of wild grapes.) "What does this feel like?" (The rough bark of an oak tree.) Even without a blindfold, there is a great deal to be learned by listening, smelling, and touching.

Vegetation is often distinctive near the water. Another day, while walking along the Delaware River, a ranger introduced us to a plant that has an interesting relationship to the fish life in the river. The shadbush, a small tree, has long pointed buds that blossom into clusters of white, long-petaled flowers in late April or early May, just as the shad are making their yearly migration up the river. The Indians were well aware of this coincidence of nature. When the shadbush bloomed, they headed for the river to throw out their nets to catch the silvery fish. Later in the year, when its berries mature, the shadbush (also called serviceberry or juneberry) provides a valuable food source for bears and other animals.

Observing an Aquatic Environment

Such outdoor biology lessons with the rangers can be translated into streamside observations you can make yourself in your home neighborhood. Walk along a flowing stream, for example, and observe how the aquatic life adapts to the current, how the tiny water animals are able to swim strongly against the current or find ways to cling to the rocks or plants so they will not be swept away. Sit at the edge of a pond and note how the shoreline plants not only provide food for animals that come to the water's edge but also create numerous hiding and lurking places for invertebrates, insects, and fish.

To get close to the animals, plants, and fish life in a river or a lake, there is no substitute for getting out on the water yourself. On many scenic rivers and lakes—as on streams in your home neighborhood—a canoe may provide the best opportunities to view the natural scene around you. Whitewater rafting and tubing offer group thrills and excitement on a river, but they have a basic drawback for natural history observation: you cannot easily control the motion that sweeps you downstream and it is difficult to beach your raft or tube to go ashore for a look around.

In a canoe, on the other hand, you can drift with the current or move against it, backpaddling or guiding the craft to the bank. Should you spot something interesting, you can do a quick binocular scan or debark and explore the riverbank. Since it draws only a few inches of water, a canoe is capable of pulling into side channels or marshy areas along the stream.

A canoe and its occupants can move through the water quietly, with no distraction to the wildlife, while a powerboat will most likely spook the animals and birds with its noisy engine. Plus, in a canoe you become more intimately involved with the wildlife around you. Since you are at the same level as many of the birds and animals, you feel yourself more a part of their world.

Stop paddling from time to time and look and listen carefully. Part of the charm of river canoeing is that you can leave the nois-

iness of everyday life behind you. Complete silence may seem
odd to those of us accustomed to having sounds all around us,
but animals are sensitive to unusual sounds and will flee from
them. Listen for a bird's call, a squirrel's chatter, or a loon's
mournful yodel. Also, keep an eye on the riverbank or the shore
of a lake for animal signs: the den a mink or muskrat has excavated into a riverbank, an otter slide, a beaver's dam, a bird's nest in
a tree, raccoon tracks on a beach.

Where to Go

To choose a river or lake that will lend itself to nature observation, scan the list of wild and scenic rivers and lakes in Appendix
B. The rivers on this list were awarded their designation by
Congress or by the states because most are free-flowing rivers
whose corridors still remain largely in their natural condition.

To better assess the rivers and lakes in your area you might
join a nature center or become a member of a canoe club. Staff
members at a nature center are usually familiar with the preserved habitats in their area. Canoeists generally know from
their own experience which canoeing streams offer good observation possibilities. If a river is canoeable, chances are that at
least one commercial canoe rental outfitter operates on the river
and can provide useful information as well as rent you a canoe.

Your local library, of course, should be a help. Several guide-
books on canoeing and rafting streams have been published. One
is *Canoeing and Rafting: The Complete Where-to-Go Guide to America's Best Tame and Wild Waters* by Sara Pyle (William Morrow,
New York, 1979). It gives a brief description of popular canoeing
and rafting rivers and provides the names of outfitters.

When you have decided on the river or lake you want to
explore, a good map is a must. The well-known topographic
maps published by the U. S. Geological Survey may be useful.
These accurate contour maps divide the entire nation into small
quadrangles. On the most detailed maps (one inch equals two
thousand feet), the ones you will probably want, the area covered is between forty-nine and sixty-four square miles. The quadrangle map you choose will show you the lay of the land and the
location of cliffs, rapids and waterfalls, as well as man-made
structures such as bridges, piers, dams, and roads.

To obtain a "topo map" of your destination, you will need to order an index of the state where the river or lake lies, then order the specific quadrangle map you desire. The index is free; each of the quadrangle maps costs $2.50. Order yours from the Map Distribution Section, U. S. Geological Survey, Federal Center, Box 25286, Denver, CO 80225.

Some highly regarded canoeing, kayaking, or rafting rivers have their own detailed river guides. We used an excellent one for our trip on the Colorado River. *The Colorado River in the Grand Canyon* by Larry Stevens, printed on 110 waterproof pages, not only displays a mile-by-mile page map of the river noting all the rapids and points of interest, it also includes informative narratives about biology and ecology, weather and climate, geology, human history, the Glen Canyon Dam, hints for private river runners, and a list of commercial river companies.

Recreational Variety

The study of nature is not the only benefit that attracts people to America's inland waters. For many a body of water exerts a magnetic pull that draws them to a river or a lake. It may be to walk along its edge, canoe it, or float down it in a raft. It may be to unfurl a fishing line or simply to watch the ceaseless movement of a stream or admire the beauty of the sun setting into a shining lake.

Such therapeutic effects were attested to by the author Zane Grey, who wrote his earliest articles and novels in a home that overlooked the Delaware River. An avid fisherman as well as an admirer of the Old West, he once put into words the deep satisfaction he felt when he heard "the deep faraway sound" of his favorite trout stream.

"The solitude of the woods, the roar of the rapids, roused the strange haunting sense of rest, of solitude, of indefinable aloofness from the tumult of the world," he wrote. "There was the wild quickening leap of the blood, the inexplicable selfish gratification of possession. The dark forest with its dank odor of decayed leaves, of wet earth, of rooting stumps was mine, all mine, as were the rush and roar of rapids, the boom of the deep falls, the hollow laugh of the low ones."

Rivers and lakes offer an escape valve for the tensions of modern life: a picnic along the banks as you watch the river slide by; poking along a lake edge in your canoe as you look for a muskrat den; the thrill of seeing your line jerk as a fish nips that artificial fly you felt sure it would go for—these are antidotes to the overload of everyday living.

If you are more devoted to participation than relaxation, wild and scenic rivers provide some of the last remaining opportunities for a real wilderness adventure. Whitewater rafting enthusiasts sign up months ahead of time to ride a raft down a surging river. Some of the most popular rafting trips in the West take participants down the Colorado River in Arizona and Utah,

The Versatile Ranger

As you visit national parks, wildlife refuges, national forests, and public lands you will cross paths with a number of the professionals whose job it is to conserve these natural areas.

Duties and job titles vary, reflecting the differing missions of the National Park Service, U. S. Fish and Wildlife Service, U. S. Forest Service, and Bureau of Land Management. National Park Service employees are known as rangers; in the U. S. Fish and Wildlife Service they are biologists, refuge managers, outdoor recreation planners, and biological technicians; in the U. S. Forest Service they are mostly foresters or forest technicians; and at the Bureau of Land Management they are biologists, resource specialists, engineers, and recreation specialists. Beyond these job titles there are several distinctions among these natural resource professionals wearing the uniforms and insignia of their individual agencies.

In the National Park Service a ranger may be trained as a resource management ranger, an interpretive ranger, or a law enforcement ranger. Such specialties reflect the Park Service mission of preserving 356 outstanding natural and man-made landmarks and interpreting their scenic values and historic significance for the public. At national park areas where the main natural resource is a river or a lake, rangers organize a variety of activities that include canoe the Salmon River in Idaho, and the Green River in Utah. In the East, rivers like the Lehigh and the Youghiogheny in Pennsylvania, the New River in West Virginia, and the Chattooga in Georgia offer exciting excursions.

Recreation planners calculate that the eighteen whitewater rivers in the eastern United States that offer raft trips draw no less than one million visitors a year who spend some $110 million in the nearby river towns and counties.

"Recreational use of our rivers and streams is increasing rapidly and new attention to protecting these opportunities is

---

trips, ranger-guided boat trips, environmental education experiences, and shoreline walks and talks to give visitors an understanding of these water re-sources. Exhibits, films, and displays add to the visitors' knowledge.

Other rangers, skilled in conservation, manage the natural resources of the park, performing water-quality tests for example. Law enforcement rangers are trained to control the large numbers of people who enjoy the parks every year, enforcing regulations both on and off the water. Seasonal rangers—the rangers you typically see at entrance stations or leading canoe trips—work for the Park Service during the peak visitor season. Rangers also provide emergency help and safety tips.

It is always a good idea to go to a park's visitor center and check in with the ranger on duty before you start a canoe or rafting trip. Rangers will inform you of any guided canoe trips that you might join to take advantage of commentary by a ranger. Check the bulletin board or the park newspaper for campfire talks on topics that interest you and take in the exhibits and film presentations at the center.

If you tell the ranger your plans, he or she may give you valuable tips on the most likely places along the river to view animals, birds, or fish, provide you with a list of wildlife and plantlife within the park, and tell you what you can expect to see at that particular season of the year. The ranger might even know of recent wildlife sightings along the river or lake.

needed," stated the President's Commission on Americans Outdoors. The commission, which in 1986 completed a thorough
study of the nation's recreation needs, called water resources
such as rivers and lakes "a backdrop for most of our recreational
activities." Fortunately for most Americans, a river or lake is
within easy reach for their benefit and enjoyment.

Within the Fish and Wildlife Service 455 national wildlife
refuges and twenty-eight wetland management districts conserve, protect, and enhance fish and wildlife and their habitats.
Professional staffs at the refuges manage the populations of bird,
animals, and fish that live in these preserves. Most of the refuges
are open to the public for wildlife-related activities such as
wildlife observation, photography, hiking, fishing, and hunting—
but not for camping or other recreation. They usually have a visitor center or contact station where a staff member or volunteer
provides information. Refuges also provide self-guiding tour roads
and nature trails, as well as observation towers for viewing migratory birds, fish, and mammals. Staff members often carry out
environmental education study programs with nearby schools
and universities. Refuge managers and their staffs monitor wildlife
populations, improve habitat, encourage wildlife propagation,
carry out research to protect the species, and enforce refuge regulations.

Although protection of wildlife is a primary objective of the
wildlife refuges, it is but one dimension of the Forest Service mission. The foresters, biologists, and range conservationists manage timber sales, maintain watersheds that provide water for
nearby towns and cities, and supervise grazing lands for live-
stock as well as protect the wild and scenic rivers that flow
through the 156 national forests, nineteen national grasslands,
thirteen national recreation areas, twenty-one national game
refuges, and other areas administered by the Forest Service.

National forests also offer extensive recreation facilities:
swimming, boating, fishing, pleasure driving, hiking, off-road
vehicle driving, horseback riding, skiing, snowmobiling, wildlife
watching, hunting, and camping. Where recreation facilities have
been developed, interpretive specialists often guide walks and
give talks at visitor centers and campgrounds.

The Bureau of Land Management oversees almost one hundred river segments on public lands in the western United States,
providing a variety of outdoor recreational opportunities such as

wildlife viewing, fishing, whitewater rafting, hunting, and sight-seeing. The Bureau's resource specialists strive to balance the diverse public demands for the use of these riparian lands with management practices that will best preserve them.

As you explore a scenic river or a lakeshore that is preserved for public use keep one point firmly in mind: In these protected areas nature calls the tune. Man may enter but needs to tread lightly, observing the natural processes but not interrupting them.

In these preserves mammals, fish, amphibians, shellfish, insects, even tiny invertebrates are allowed to complete their life cycles without interference. They forage for their food, prey and are preyed upon, and reproduce their young — all undisturbed. Each creature must find its own niche in the food chain.

You and I have the privilege of enjoying these protected rivers and lakes as long as we fit into this natural web. We need to blend into the background while we enjoy the beauty of the scene as our canoe slides downstream. We should pick our way through the marsh grass, careful not to flush the bird life we know is there. In this way we can share with the early explorers like Lewis and Clark the thrill they must have felt when they experienced these rivers and lakes for the first time.

CHAPTER
2

How Rivers and Lakes Get Their Start

RIVERS

The warm rain pelted the surface of the river, producing small bubbles that soon melted away. Water dripped in front of our faces from the hoods of our rain suits although the full-length plastic suits kept us dry underneath— everything, that is, except our feet.

A man and his son, their fishing interrupted by the steady rain, were just pulling their canoe ashore as we slid our two canoes into the stream. Quizzical looks followed us as the three of us shoved off into the current. We were determined, however, that no rain, even a steady one, would keep us from accepting the invitation of Dennis Kaleta, a National Park Service ranger, to canoe part of the Namekagon River, a major tributary of the St. Croix National Scenic Riverway, which forms part of the border between Wisconsin and Minnesota.

"I hardly ever get a chance to canoe in the rain," Dennis confided. "Oddly enough, I really enjoy it. There's never anyone else on the river and the woods are so quiet."

He was right. We saw no other person as we paddled this wilderness river. Even the birds were silent. The only sounds we heard were the drip of the rain from the bushes and trees, our own hushed voices, and the gentle swish of our paddle blades as we stroked our way downstream.

By the end of the afternoon our canoes had gathered a good bit of rainwater, but our heads had gathered many basic facts about rivers. Rivers, we discovered, collect their water from four sources—and the Namekagon on this wet day was being swelled by three of them.

The first source, of course, is the rain that falls directly into the river, the raindrops that today pocked its surface (and occasionally ran down our necks). Although this is not a major source of water supply for rivers, it can be a significant one for lakes with large surface areas.

The second source is the runoff water we saw trickling in rivulets down the banks and into the river. A rainfall or snowfall, Dennis explained, saturates the ground until it cannot hold any more. Then the rain, unable to be absorbed, runs over the ground surface and eventually into a river or lake. Runoff also occurs when the rain falls too fast to be absorbed, as in a sudden downpour, or when the rain falls on a nonabsorbent surface such as leaf litter on a forest floor.

The bowl-shaped area that collects the rainwater destined for a river or lake is called a drainage basin or watershed. One drainage basin is separated from another by a high ridge of land called a divide. The streams that form within a basin to carry water to the main river are called tributaries. Tributaries grow in size as they converge on the main stem of the river they feed. The volume of a river depends on the area of its drainage basin and the amount of rain that falls into it. The vast Mississippi River drainage basin, the third largest in the world, includes more than 1,245,000 square miles that cover thirty-one states and two Canadian provinces.

The third source that added water to the Namekagon was one we could not see. Besides the visible surface water, other water from below ground was increasing the volume of the river on this rainy afternoon. Underground reservoirs of groundwater are built up as precipitation from the surface filters down through the soil until it meets a watertight layer of bedrock. As the subterranean water accumulates it fills all openings and cracks in the rocks and soil.

The top level of this underground saturated zone is called the water table. The depth of the water table beneath the surface varies with the amount of precipitation and the climate. In humid regions the water table may be only a few feet below the ground. In a desert it may be a hundred or even thousands of feet down. The saturated layer between the bedrock below and the water table is called an aquifer. Water from an aquifer often seeps directly into a river, thereby augmenting its flow. Groundwater is often held in an aquifer for a long time before it comes to the surface, sometimes hundreds or even thousands of years. This seep-age from below ground sustains the flow of many rivers that would be reduced to a trickle if they depended only on the direct input from rainfall and runoff.

Groundwater may reappear as a spring, perhaps a spring that is the source of a river. Under certain conditions it may reach the surface even more dramatically as an artesian well, a spring that bursts forth like a natural fountain. If the groundwater comes in contact with a heat source such as volcanic activity, it may spurt to the surface as a geyser.

The fourth way that rivers (although not the Namekagon) collect water is from the meltwater of glaciers and snowfields high in the mountains. The Columbia River of the Pacific Northwest, which originates in the mountains of British Columbia, gets a large part of its flow from melting ice and snow.

The Hydrologic Cycle

This precipitation that fills rivers and lakes is dependent upon a worldwide phenomenon known as the hydrologic cycle. Throughout the earth's history the same water has been used and reused, frozen, melted, evaporated, condensed, and carried from one location to another by the forces of nature.

When it rains, sleets, hails, or snows, the resulting water finds its way into the world's oceans, rivers, and lakes or beneath the ground to remain for a time as groundwater. When the sun warms the earth's surface, moisture from the 70 percent of the surface that is covered with water evaporates into the air as water vapor. Trees and plants add to the vapor in the air through transpiration, giving off water vapor through tiny pores in their leaves.

This remarkable cycle completes itself as the water vapor comes in contact with microscopic particles of dust and salt suspended in the air and condenses to form clouds. As further condensation occurs, the droplets grow larger until their weight causes them to fall to the earth as rain or snow.

The Little Salmon River in central Idaho changes its personality to fit the terrain beneath it. In its upper course the stream meanders through a flat meadowland; later, as the gradient steepens, the river tumbles through a rock-strewn valley.

Rivers Change Character

A river displays different characteristics as it flows from its source to its outlet. In its upper reaches the slope of its channel (called the gradient) is steep, usually more than fifty feet of height to a mile of length. Tumbling water leaps over waterfalls and surges through rapids as it carves a deepening channel between steep banks. Its current is swift and carries with it sand and gravel, sometimes even sizable rocks. This combination of grit and fast-flowing water can literally "sandpaper" a ravine through soil and rocks that stand in the way.

In its middle course a river leaves the steeper slopes of the mountains to enter lower lands where the slope is more gradual, usually no more than ten feet to the mile. As the river widens and the flow slows, the river drops most of the material it has carried down from the mountains, creating gravelly beds on the channel bottom. Sand or gravel bars form in the river as this silt and sand swirls into heaps; when these deposits build up above the water surface they become islands that can support vegetation.

As a river flows through its lower course the accumulation of silt causes its bottom to become shallower. Now its gradient is only a few inches for every mile of length. The river flow slows as it makes its way through a wide, flat valley or across a coastal plain. A slow-flowing river does not have the power to carve deeply into the land. Instead, it tends to meander, curving like a snake across the flatlands.

At the end of its journey a river drops any remaining sediment into a bay or ocean, forming a delta—a sandy, fanlike triangle of land at the river mouth. In the case of the Mississippi so much silt has accumulated near its mouth that the level of the river is higher than the surrounding countryside. Engineers have constructed massive earthen levees in an attempt to hold the river within its banks and forestall widespread flooding.

At the mouth of other rivers the combined action of the river's flow and the ocean tides, instead of forming a delta, scoops out the river's mouth. If the sea tides carry away some of the silt from the river's mouth, it becomes a broad estuary that provides an excellent protected harbor for shipping. The Hudson River, for example, empties into the estuary that is New York's harbor.

Erosion at Work

An elementary but important fact to keep in mind is that water is surprisingly heavy. A garden pail full of water weighs some seventeen pounds. Fill a large bathtub and it will weigh three-quarters of a ton.

When water is in motion, this weight, added to its momentum, creates a great force. Hydrologists—the scientists who specialize in the behavior of water—calculate that the force of water increases by the square of its velocity. Thus the force exerted is four times greater when water is moving at ten miles per hour than when it is moving at five miles per hour.

The power of a river to cut its way through the terrain is nowhere more dramatically evident than at the Grand Canyon of the Colorado River. Outdoor enthusiasts riding one of the popular rafts down the river admire the steep canyon walls that have been shaped by the river's powerful erosive action.

Erosion by a river takes three forms. Hydraulic action from the sheer weight of the water pushes soil particles, sand, pebbles, and even rocks downstream. Abrasive action by these particles scours and deepens the stream bed. Finally, chemical action of the water dissolves minerals from rocks and soil and mixes them into the water as salts.

We saw a dramatic example of the power of water erosion the day we walked through Watkins Glen, a gorge at the head of thirty-eight-mile-long Seneca Lake in the Finger Lakes region of New York State. The erosion at Watkins Glen took place some twelve thousand years ago when great glaciers extended down from Canada over what is now the upper Midwest and New England states. As the glaciers melted, torrents of meltwater poured down the flanks of the sheets of ice forming rushing streams that cut chasms through the sedimentary rock.

We sensed the tremendous cutting power of this Ice Age meltwater as we walked through the chasm along with some of the thousands of tourists who visit Watkins Glen each year. The vertical rock walls soar three hundred feet upward to the ground surface and are so close together that in places they keep the sunlight from reaching the bottom of the canyon.

As you walk the trail that winds along the gorge wall you pass through tunnels in the rock, beneath towering cliffs, and under a waterfall that cascades over your head. As the mile-and-a-half-long trail squeezes through the narrow chute of water called a flume you view eighteen other waterfalls or cascades that range from straight drops over a cliff to twisted chutes where the rock has been polished by the running water to the texture and color of mahogany.

Perhaps the most vivid evidence we saw of the erosive action of the ancient river was a series of potholes, symmetrically rounded depressions in the rock floor of the chasm. These depressions, some the size of a wash basin, others the size of a bathtub, were scoured out by stones and gravel that were swirled at high speeds by the force of the surging water. The swirling stones ground holes into the bedrock like a giant augur biting into the surface.

Today only a gently flowing stream runs along the floor of the glen, continuing to deepen this chasm that was so dramatically carved many years ago by the force of the raging glacial meltwater.

Flooding

Heavy spring rains or snow melting in nearby mountains causes a river to swell. If it is a "young" river that flows through a deep canyon, the increased volume of water causes the crest to climb higher up the canyon walls while the river cuts deeper into its bed.

But if it is an "old" river that flows through a broad valley, its waters will rise until they overflow its banks, expanding outward onto the valley floor or flood plain. The flood plain absorbs some of the floodwater, collecting it in temporary lakes that allow it to flow gradually back into the river or seep into the ground to add to the underground water.

Such flooding can produce benefits as well as problems. Silt from the muddy floodwaters settle out, building up the topsoil. As a result, floodplains form some of the most productive agricultural land in the country. But in the United States, as in other countries, a number of cities and towns have been established on river floodplains. Such a location may seem beneficial for agriculture, commerce, or transportation reasons, but it is risky because of potential flooding. Officials estimate that in the United States about 3,800 settlements with a population of 2,500 or more are vulnerable to flooding. The Mississippi, Missouri, and Ohio river systems are among the principal flood areas in the country.

Engineers have tirelessly devised methods to fend off the seasonal floodwaters. They have erected huge dams to hold back the floods, constructed diversion channels to carry excess water away, built levees and embankments to contain the torrents, and dredged silt from riverbeds to deepen the channels. No less than fifty thousand large dams now affect every major river or their tributaries in the lower forty-eight states except for the Salmon River in Idaho and the Yellowstone River in Wyoming and Montana.

But effective flood control measures begin far upstream from where the dams and levees are usually built. How a farmer plows his land, what crops he plants, and how he controls the drainage on his land contribute directly to how much storm water is absorbed by his land, and therefore how much runs off into the river. So does the vegetation that grows along a river's upper reaches. Each blade of grass absorbs some of the rain or snow runoff that accumulates into a flood. The water seeps down into the ground and is held there by roots and decayed vegetation.

In heavily wooded areas or in grasslands, light showers may never hit the ground before being intercepted by the vegetation. In addition, the roots of trees and other plants—even the tiny tunnels created by worms—break the surface of the ground and allow rainfall to trickle below ground.

But when the land is plowed or stripped of vegetation, the rain runs off readily, carrying away much of the topsoil. Such erosive action allows more rainwater to run off than can be absorbed. The runoff carries soil from the land to the river or stream in the form of silt. Silt raises the bed of a river, making it shallower and therefore more apt to flood the next time. Silt also builds up behind a dam, decreasing its effective height and lessening the amount of water it can hold back.

The type of surface the rain falls on also has a lot to do with how much runoff will end up in a river. Sandy soil, or humus, will absorb more water than will dense clay. Clay, in turn, will absorb more than a paved surface. When spread across a land surface, concrete and asphalt act as shields against infiltration so most rainfall will run off immediately into sewers or ditches to make its way toward the nearest river.

One type of flood that is especially hard to predict (and hard to escape) is the flash flood. These rapidly developing floods occur when a sudden cloudburst unleashes tons of rainwater on a relatively small area too fast to be absorbed, turning small streams into raging torrents and filling dry washes with runoff water.

For example, on July 31, 1976, a line of thunderstorms stalled over an area north of Denver, dumping from two to five inches of rain an hour. Nearby creeks, rising rapidly, fed their water into steep-sided Big Thompson Canyon. The Big Thompson River rose twenty feet, its waters racing through the canyon at twenty feet per second. The sudden deluge overwhelmed campers in the canyon and motorists on the roads. The force of the water even washed away an entire motel—and its twenty-three guests.

Riverbank Vegetation

A forest of trees is the best friend a watershed can have. All the forestlands of the United States, a hydrologist estimated, receive an average of forty-two inches of rain a year and yield some seventeen inches of that in annual runoff. Were all this runoff used, it would provide Americans with a daily supply of water exceeding 1.1 trillion gallons.

The rainfall that does not run off seeps into the ground to become groundwater, evaporates, or is used to sustain the trees and plants of the forests. If fires or logging operations strip the watershed of trees and other vegetation, this water collection system is destroyed. No trees and plants remain to intercept the raindrops on their fall to the ground or to protect the bare soil from their impact. Lack of undergrowth or leaf cover on the ground allows the runoff to quickly form rivulets that grow into gullies in the soft soil and pluck the soil from its bed.

The exposed soil turns to mud. With nothing to anchor it to the slope, it begins to slide downward. The result is not only a faster runoff of water but also a rapid dissolving of the soil into a mud slide that can wipe out everything in its path. Mudslides on barren California slopes have carried away entire houses and sliced through streets.

Several Bureau of Land Management employees in Wyoming once hit upon a novel way to prevent the erosion of a stream bank. Knowing there was a group of beavers in the area, they hauled in a number of slim willow and aspen logs and left them near the stream site. As they hoped, the beavers set to work, using the readily available building material to construct a series of dams that slowed the flooding and gained enough time for vegetation to grow and thereby stabilize the stream banks.

Forests and vegetation along a river preserve the river setting in a number of ways. Vegetation filters the rainfall, absorbing the nutrients for its own growth. It helps retain the moisture, traps silt and organic matter, and prevents the rapid runoff that would carry soil and debris into the river. Vegetation plays an important role in flood control by absorbing flood waters and releasing them slowly, thus preventing floods from overwashing the land and stripping it bare. Forested riverbanks also provide essential breeding, nesting, and feeding habitats for many species of wildlife and waterfowl.

In the eastern United States look for silver maple, black willow, sycamore, butternut, swamp white oak, and American hornbeam among the trees that grow well around water. An Indian favorite was the paper birch; the early inhabitants peeled the bark from it to make their birchbark canoes. In the Midwest you can often tell where the streams and water courses are located by the cottonwood trees that grow there. In the Southeast water oak, willow oak, tupelo, and bald cypress are familiar specimens on riverbanks or in wetlands. In the Northwest, cedars commonly grow along streams.

LAKES

A lake is normally a manifestation of the water table beneath the ground. It forms in a natural depression that dips below the level of saturation of the underlying aquifer.

Lakes obtain their water from the same sources as rivers: from direct rainfall, runoff of surface water, groundwater seepage, and, in northern areas, from glaciers and snowfields. But whereas a river is an active participant in its formation, continuing to cut its own path, a lake is usually the result of an external force that created it.

Some lakes are formed by shifts deep within the earth's crust. The world's deepest lake, Lake Baikal in the Soviet Union, was created in this way. Lake Baikal is so large and deep that it is calculated to hold fully one-fifth of the world's fresh water. In 1812 an earthquake shook the Mississippi Valley. The quake was so powerful that areas of land sank as much as ten feet. Among the lakes formed by this quake was Reelfoot Lake, now a popular recreational lake along the Tennessee-Kentucky border.

Yet another way that a lake can appear is as the result of a lava flow or a rock slide that blocks the flow of a river. For example, when Mount St. Helens volcano erupted in 1980 in the Cascade Range of Washington, several new lakes were created.

Most of the numerous lakes in the north-central and northeast part of the country were formed by the scraping action of the glaciers that receded from these regions ten to twelve thousand years ago. The sheer weight of this overburden of ice, combined with the grinding action of boulders embedded in it, stripped away the soil and scooped out shallow bowls in the bedrock. As the vast ice sheets melted, the water filled these depressions. Deposits of rock and sand dropped by the glaciers dammed up existing rivers to form other lakes. Another type of lake, the kettle lake, formed when huge chunks of ice left behind by the retreating glacier melted like giant ice cubes to make a depression in the surface, which then filled with its own meltwater.

Still another type, an oxbow lake, occurs when water is left behind by the changing course of a river. Oxbows are found in broad floodplains where a river meanders, forming almost complete loops with only a narrow neck of land separating each loop. When the river floods, water takes the shortest route and gushes across the narrow neck of land, creating a new channel. When the floodwaters recede, the river uses the new channel instead of the old loop. The floodwater stays behind in the crescent-shaped oxbow and is later supplemented with rainwater or groundwater.

Another type of lake forms as the result of chemical action. This type is the sinkhole, usually found in regions where a layer

Vegetation is the victor when a lake dies. At Pinhook Bog within Indiana Dunes National Lakeshore, Ranger Darryl Blink describes to Marge how sphagnum moss and other vegetation, creeping gradually inward from the edges, will eventually smother the pond, ending its existence.

of limestone lies near the surface. Water beneath the ground dissolves the limestone above it, causing the terrain above to collapse into the cavity, exposing the water below. Sinkholes are common in the inland part of the Florida peninsula.

Lakes have been created, too, by man's action. On many of the nation's rivers, agencies have built dams that block a river's flow, backing up water to form an artificial lake—the familiar reservoir. The two largest reservoirs of this kind, measured by acre-feet of water impounded, are Lake Mead between Arizona and Nevada (created by Hoover Dam) and Lake Powell in Utah (created by the Glen Canyon Dam). Both reservoirs are formed from the flow of the Colorado River.

Lakes Grow Old

Unlike rivers, which are constantly in motion and renew themselves, lakes are passive bodies of water that "grow old." A lake, trapped in its basin, gradually fills with sediment and plant matter and eventually is transformed into dry land.

Occasionally a lake might come to a more sudden end. An earthquake can drain a lake quickly, just as a quake can be the force that creates one. On a visit to Rocky Mountain National Park we observed where several lakes had disappeared overnight. We looked down into a stream valley where beavers had previously built several dams. The resulting lakes had formed watery stairsteps in the sloping valley. But now the lakes were gone after a spring flood had swept aside sections of the dams and the stream had resumed its normal course.

Usually, however, a lake grows old gracefully. If nature is left undisturbed, this slow process has a number of steps. In a young lake the water is clear, rich in dissolved oxygen, and free of elements such as nitrogen and phosphorus that encourage plant growth. During its early years minerals begin to enter the lake, leaching into the water from surrounding rocks and soil, flowing in from tributary streams, or dropping in with rainfall.

As the mineral content increases, the nutrients allow algae to grow. The algae makes use of sunlight to convert the nutrients into food through photosynthesis. The blooms of algae, like grass on a prairie, provide good grazing for a whole host of tiny water animals, such as water fleas and small crustaceans, called zooplankton. Fish feed on the zooplankton or on plants growing on the shallow lake bottom along the shore, insect larvae, and other small creatures. The fish themselves now become part of the food chain. Otters seek them out for a meal. So do birds of prey and land animals such as bears.

As a lake reaches old age, more and more nutrients promote the growth of rooted plants in the shallows. Algae spreads to cover the entire surface, giving the lake the appearance of a giant bowl of pea soup. Its waters fill with increasing amounts of decaying vegetation. Sediments from the decaying plants gradually build up on the lake bottom, decreasing the depth of the water. New plants take root in the shallower water and die, leaving behind their organic remains as a fertile bed for the next season's plants.

Vegetation covering the lake surface calms the wave action generated by wind blowing across the lake, thus cutting down on the absorption of oxygen into the water. Oxygen is also extracted from the water by plants and fish.

The fish life changes. Instead of the lake trout and whitefish that like clear, cold water, the aging lake holds bass and sunfish that thrive in the shallower waters that have grown warmer from exposure to sunlight.

Man sometimes hastens the death of a lake by adding organic materials—grass clippings, leaves, garbage, sewage, or industrial wastes—that consume even more of the dwindling oxygen supply. Phosphorus and nitrates contained in the runoff from farms and homes fertilize the vegetation in a lake just as they fertilize a farm or residence.

In this slow process, called *eutrification*, the lake fills in after many years, becoming a marsh or bog. After another period of years the bog firms into solid ground that gives few hints of the lake that once lay there.

We explored such a marshy area the morning we joined Seasonal Ranger Darryl Blink to investigate Pinhook Bog, a unique marsh that lies several miles inland from Lake Michigan within the boundary of Indiana Dunes National Lakeshore. Pinhook Bog is the remnant of a lake that was left behind thousands of years ago when the last glaciers retreated from this part of Indiana. It is such a remarkable area that it has been designated as a national natural landmark, a habitat duplicated in few if any other places in the country.

As the lake grew older, Darryl related, vegetation including sphagnum moss began to grow inward from its edges, eventually spreading across the lake's surface. Sphagnum, the familiar peat moss that gardeners use to mulch bushes and plants, is a ground-hugging plant that can hold ten to twenty times its weight in water.

As the spreading mat of sphagnum covered the former lake, it became thicker. Soon it could support small plants, then larger plants such as poison sumac, black chokecherry, high-bush blueberry, mountain holly, and winterberry. Today the mat of vegetation is firm enough to support even twenty-foot trees.

Darryl, who is a social studies teacher for most of the year and a park interpreter during the summer, told us of the unusual plants that grow in this natural botanical garden: a variety of ferns, leatherleaf, bog rosemary, cranberry, and blueberry bushes that have adapted to the acidic environment where both the oxygen and nutrient levels are very low.

When we reached a boardwalk that led into the bog, it seemed as though we were heading into a green tunnel. Light green carpets of sphagnum spread beneath the planks. Ground cover and tiny flowers grew luxuriantly from the dark ooze. Bushes and shrubs, growing as high as our heads, reached over the boardwalk with their branches. We were enveloped by a coolness that contrasted with the warm, midmorning temperatures we had left. Droplets of moisture covered the leaves and flowers, defying the efforts of shafts of sunlight to dry them.

"It's always cooler here because the vegetation is evaporating so much moisture," Darryl explained. He stooped to point out a sundew plant, one of the unusual carnivorous plants that live here. Its reddish leaves secrete a sticky nectar that attracts insects to the plant. When its prey lands on a leaf, the plant closes a cluster of leaves like sticky fingers over the unlucky insect, then consumes the insect, digesting it through its leaves.

Another carnivorous species, the pitcher plant, accomplishes the same thing using a slightly different method. Its reddish purple leaves curl into a tubelike shape, or pitcher, forming an insect trap. Raindrops fall into this opening and collect in its base.

Tiny honey glands that cover the outside surface of the pitcher give off a sweet smell that attracts insects to the opening. When one lands near the lip of the pitcher, bristly hairs nudge it into the opening and the insect slides into the cup where it drowns in the syrupy water at its base. The plant later digests the insect, thereby absorbing nitrogen that it needs but is unable to get from the bog through its root system.

We stopped to look at a small tamarack tree. Its needles look similar to those of other members of the pine family, but the tamarack, unlike other pines, is deciduous, dropping its needles in the winter instead of holding on to them like an evergreen. The Indians, Darryl said, used the tough roots of the tamarack to bind together their birchbark canoes.

At the end of the boardwalk we reached a clearing. Darryl invited us to step off the boardwalk onto the dark brown surface. Marge did—and looked up with surprise. "It's springy," she laughed as she bounced gently, "like stepping onto a mattress!"

When she stood still, her shoes were soon outlined with water seeping around them. Even when she stepped to one side, her footprints remained outlined by the water.

"You're standing atop a ten-foot layer of decayed sphagnum moss that has accumulated here over many years," Darryl said. "A crop of sphagnum grows, then dies, and a new crop of moss grows on top of it."

"Actually," he chuckled, "you're walking on water. The thick mat of sphagnum where you're standing is floating on the water of the former lake. Under the ten feet of moss is another thirty-five feet of water down to the bottom of the lake!"

When Marge jumped up and down gently on the sphagnum surface, fifteen-foot trees nearby showed the effect, bending toward us. "Don't poke a hole in the surface," Darryl warned, "or water will ooze up through it."

In a scientific experiment a botanist in 1940 had done just that, Darryl said. Seeking to define the history of the bog, he used a hollow bore and drove it down through the bog, sampling the material he found at every foot level. Taking his samples back to his university laboratory, he analyzed the tree pollen he found at each level. From the pollen he determined the plants that grew at each period of the history of the bog and what the climate was. From these clues he concluded that the bog began with a cold, moist climate that favored fir and spruce, then gave way to a cool but drier climate that favored jack and white pine, and finally led to a warmer, drier climate that favored oak and hickory.

Only in a bog such as this—or perhaps in the frozen icecap of Antarctica—would pollen be sufficiently preserved to tell this vegetative history spanning thousands of years. The thick mat of sphagnum cuts off the water below from oxygen. The combination of highly acid water with low oxygen content and few minerals inhibit the growth of bacteria. With little bacteria to act upon it, the vegetative mat of the bog decays very slowly as it continues to thicken.

"The bog is a fragile environment and we treat it accordingly," Darryl said. "This is the only place along the boardwalk where we allow visitors to step onto the sphagnum layer. Usually, of course, we ask people to stay off it. But only by getting the sensation, as you have, would you understand what a unique environment this bog represents."

CHAPTER
3

Appalachians and Eastern Woodlands

RIVERS

Many a river in the eastern United States begins life as a trickle high in the Appalachian Mountains, the forested range that marches diagonally across the landscape from Maine to Georgia.

Accumulating runoff from the region's abundant rainfall, the trickle swells to a torrent, then into a swiftly flowing stream that twists out of the mountains and onto the gently sloping piedmont ("foot of the mountain" in French). One stream joins another, then another, widening and gaining momentum as they flow across the piedmont and the coastal plain. Major rivers such as the Connecticut, Hudson, Delaware, Susquehanna, Potomac, and James follow roughly parallel paths as they cross the eastern seaboard to reach the Atlantic Ocean.

As the streams and rivers course through the mountains, taking the path of least resistance, they form valleys. The valleys serve as natural pathways that in various eras have guided Indians, pioneers, canal builders, railroad men, highway constructors, and marching armies. Lumberjacks in the 1800s took advantage of eastern rivers such as Maine's Kennebec to float battalions of logs downriver to sawmills and waiting schooners.

As they near the ocean, the rivers pour over a drop in elevation where the harder rock underlying the piedmont meets the softer, sedimentary rock of the coastal plain. The resulting waterfalls, cascades, and rapids at this "fall line" provided the waterpower that made possible the development of cities such as Trenton, Philadelphia, Baltimore, and Washington, D.C.

Today in New England, according to a recent nationwide inventory, only 5 percent of the total river mileage remains free-

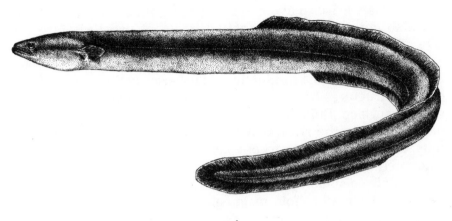

eel

flowing—and power companies want to construct hydroelectric dams on these segments as well.

Eel

The eel is a catadromous fish that lives part of its life in the salt water of the ocean and another part in the fresh water of a river. We learned about this fascinating creature on the upper Delaware River.

On a seventy-three-mile-long stretch of the river that forms the boundary between New York and Pennsylvania, the National Park Service works cooperatively with fifteen river towns and with county, state, regional, and federal agencies to preserve the natural, physical, and cultural character of the river corridor and provide a variety of river recreation. On the warm summer day we were there, sunbathers swarmed over the flat rocks along the river while squadrons of rubber rafts slid through the rapids, their occupants trying to outyell the roar of the rumbling water. Canoeists paddled in the flat water below. Both the rafters and the canoeists learn to avoid not only natural obstacles like rocks but also certain man-made structures that protrude into the river. These are the eel weirs.

Eel fishermen have long built their weirs in the Delaware River, one of the most productive eel fisheries in the world. The V-shaped structures have two wing walls that reach just above the water's surface. Built of large rocks, the walls reach more than halfway across the river, leaving only enough room for canoes, rafts, and boats to pass to one side. Fisherman Floyd Campfield recounted to us the amazing life history of the humble eel.

Female eels make their way down eastern rivers such as the Delaware each fall to join male eels that are waiting for them in the brackish water at the river's mouth. Together the eels then make a long spawning migration to the Sargasso Sea near Bermuda, which is said to be the saltiest part of the North Atlantic. Biologists have not solved all the mysteries of this epic migration. But they have discovered that the females descend as much as fifteen hundred feet beneath the ocean surface and there release as many as ten thousand eggs apiece. Then they die.

The resulting larvae, tiny and transparent, drift with the Gulf Stream toward the U. S. coast, gradually changing into immature eels. In the spring nearly a year later, one thousand miles or more from their birthplace, the young female eels swim into the river, leaving the males behind in the estuary. As the female swims up the freshwater stream it turns a yellowish green. Eating insects, larvae, and small mussels and fish, it remains in the river for seven to ten years. It grows to a length of three to four feet, eventually changing to a silvery gray as it reaches adulthood.

Shad

The erection of dams across eastern rivers changed the migration patterns of fish like the shad. Shad are anadromous (pronounced a-NA-dru-muss) fish whose life cycle is the reverse of the American eel: shad are born in the fresh water of a river but

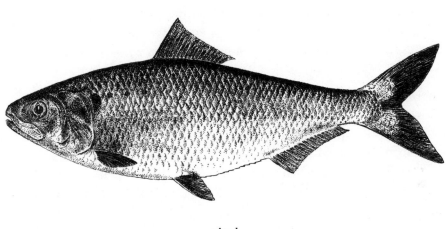

shad

live most of their lives in the salt water of the ocean. When mature, they return to the river of their birth, lay their eggs, and reproduce. They are bluish above and have silvery sides. A full-grown shad is about two feet in length and averages three pounds.

When the country's first settlers turned to the rivers as a food source, the silvery American shad, America's largest member of the herring family, filled East Coast rivers. But as dams blocked the rivers and industrial and human waste polluted the water, the shad could no longer reach their traditional spawning grounds on the upper reaches. By the early 1800s few if any survived in these overfished, industrialized, and blocked eastern rivers.

Finally, conservationists and fishermen protested. In the 1950s legislation began requiring a reduction of the wastes going into eastern rivers, thus improving the river water quality and restoring the dissolved oxygen the fish needed. Fishways were built that allowed migrating fish to bypass the dams and continue upstream to spawn.

The American shad, responding to these improved conditions, have resumed their spawning runs in many eastern rivers. Beginning in February in the rivers of Florida and continuing through June in the rivers of Maine, the silvery fish head upriver. The number of shad migrating up the Delaware River, for example, increased from approximately 200,000 in 1975 to 850,000 in 1989 according to the U. S. Fish and Wildlife Service, which takes a census each year.

In their run upstream, which usually begins toward the end of March, the shad follow a leader and seem to watch for changing conditions in the water. Joe Miller, Fish Program Coordinator of the U. S. Fish and Wildlife Service for the Delaware River Basin, tells of standing on a bridge across the Upper Delaware and observing how wary the shad are of even a change in the color of the water. When the shadow of a tree or bridge fell across the water, he said, the lead fish seemed to become confused, schooling up with its followers. Once the fish grew accustomed to the shadow, however, the leader gathered its group together once more and quickly swam past the shadowed area to continue the run upstream.

When the shad reach the upriver tributary where they will spawn, females look for locations in the shallows where there is a gravel bottom. There each female deposits thirty thousand or more eggs over which the male shad immediately spreads its milt, or sperm.

Should you find yourself near a shad spawning location in early summer, you might see and hear this reproductive ritual. You will hear the sound of splashing in the shallows as the male swims alongside the female, beating his tail against her side to encourage her to release her eggs.

In late summer some of the eggs will hatch, filling the river with silvery fingerlings. Cool autumn temperatures signal the young fish, now three to five inches long, to head downriver to the ocean where they will live and grow until the time arrives when they themselves will spawn in their ancestral river.

After spawning, the adult shad make their way back to the ocean. But they are worn out from their exertions and many die en route; only 1 or 2 percent have the energy to reach the ocean.

Merganser

The resurgence of the shad was but one of the many things we learned the day we took a ranger-led canoe trip on the Delaware River within the Delaware Water Gap National Recreation Area. At this thirty-seven-mile-long national park area that lies along both banks of the river in Pennsylvania and New Jersey, the best way to see the river is from a canoe. So we joined one of the weekly canoe trips that give visitors a paddler's-eye view of one of the last free-flowing rivers on the Atlantic coast. The expedition was led by Ranger Tara Barrett.

"Look over there," she whispered suddenly, pointing to a brown rock to our left. At first we saw nothing. Then what we thought were bumps on the rocks materialized into three ducks.

"Mergansers," Tara said. Through our binoculars we picked out the crested reddish head and gray body of a female merganser and two ducklings. The male has a long white body and dark head. "They dive beneath the water to feed on minnows, chubs, and suckers, or crustaceans and vegetation on the bottom," she told us. "But they make their nests on land, often in tree cavities or hollow snags. So a riverway like the Delaware River that runs through a woodland is just right for them."

As if on cue, the three ducks left the rock and swam across the water. One dived beneath the surface, then reappeared with something in its bill. Another—a duckling—tried unsuccessfully to fly. Flapping its wings furiously, it seemed to bicycle across the surface, slapping the water with its orange feet, then gave up and settled back onto the surface again.

When these young ducklings mature, Tara said, they will improve their feeding techniques. One trick that mergansers soon learn is to fly upstream, alight on the water, then drift along with the current as they surface-dive to find succulent prey in the water.

In places where the water shallowed out our canoes slid only inches above the rocky riverbed. Shafts of sunlight penetrated to the bottom, illuminating mussel shells and wavy strands of eel grass that provide food for the ducks and hiding places for fish such as smallmouth bass, brown trout, shiners, carp, rock bass, crappie, and sunfish. The fish feed not only on the bottom-growing plants but also on smaller fish, invertebrates, and insects.

The mergansers have found a good home on the Delaware River. On other rivers of the Northeast you may see not only mergansers but also mallards, goldeneyes, and buffleheads.

Black Bear

You will sometimes see large mammals along the riverbank, Tara said—perhaps a white-tailed deer or a black bear. A few days before we arrived, one of the rangers had spotted a black bear swimming across the river.

The black bear is mostly black, but many have a brown nose or white patches on the chest. The average black bear standing on all fours is about three feet high and five feet long, and weighs between two and three hundred pounds, although it may seem larger because of its long, coarse hair and loose skin. A bear can run as fast as twenty-five miles an hour and is a skillful tree climber as well as a competent swimmer.

Black bears spend most of their time foraging for food in the mixed hardwood and softwood forests of the eastern Appalachians. A bear's diet is largely vegetarian—berries, acorns, fruits, nuts, leaves, and roots—but it will eat meat such as amphibians, reptiles, small mammals, dead fish, insects, grubs, or human garbage if it comes across it.

Muskrat

Other animals often sighted along rivers are muskrats and mink, both of which need a watery environment to survive.

Muskrats live in burrows they dig in the riverbank or under masses of tree branches and sticks that have been washed up along the river's edge by an eddy. Sometimes the muskrat takes over the abandoned home of a beaver. Its burrow consists of a central chamber with a number of passages leading into it, all from beneath the surface to give it protection from predators like the mink.

The muskrat is about half the size of a beaver and has a rounded tail in contrast to the beaver's flat one. It makes good use of its tail to steer it through the water. To help it swim speedily, the muskrat's large hind feet have partial webbing between the toes. Its broad rounded head is attached to its body with no apparent neck. Small ears lie close to its head.

The muskrat takes its name from the musk glands at the base of its tail that it uses to add scent to its lodge, feeding platforms, and trails along the riverbank. Muskrats identify each other by these distinctive odors.

muskrat

This aquatic animal devours a wide variety of plants that live in and around the water. Its favorite foods include the roots, bulbs, tubers, stems, and leaves of sedges, cordgrass, cattails, and reeds that grow in shallow water at the river's edge. It also eats clams, fish, salamanders, turtles, crayfish, and snails. The muskrat does not store food for the winter because it can swim under the ice to feed on bottom growth. If the ice should thicken and prevent the muskrat from foraging, it has yet another option—it can eat up its own house of sticks and vegetation.

Mink

The mink, a member of the weasel family, is a double threat: agile both on land or in the water. It is about two feet long, not counting its bushy tail, and has a slender body and stubby legs. It weighs from one to two pounds. Like the river otter that it resembles, it is an excellent swimmer and can dive to depths of twenty feet before surfacing for air.

mink

In the water mink prey on fish, frogs, crayfish, snakes, crustaceans, and an occasional muskrat. On land they hunt mice, rabbits, birds, insects, and eggs. Since it has limited vision underwater, the mink usually sights its quarry from the riverbank, then dives into the water to catch it before it escapes. On land it searches between rocks, under logs, or in rodent burrows to find its next meal. Biologists say that a mink spends 90 percent of its active time hunting along the shore or in the water.

Like the muskrat, the mink possesses well-developed musk glands at the base of its tail that it uses to mark its territory. A double layer of fur keeps it warm in the water. The underfur retains its body heat while the well-oiled outer guard hairs protect the mink's coat from wear when it rubs against rocks and branches. Its thick coat has long made this riverside animal a desirable catch for fur trappers.

Your best chance to spot a mink is at dusk when the animal emerges from its home beneath a tree's roots, in a fallen log, or from a pile of rocks to begin a night's stalking. The mink is commonly found in cypress-tupelo swamps of the South and along rivers like the New River in West Virginia.

Turkey Vulture

The New River, we found, is a superb place to view a diverse array of aquatic wildlife. The river has cut a gorge averaging a thousand feet deep through the Appalachian Mountains. This section of the river is a designated national river. We had a spectacular view of the gorge the day we wedged ourselves into an inflatable rubber raft and braved the surging current—the New River boasts some of the finest whitewater in the East—guided by Hilarie Jones and Wayne Yonkelowitz, both schoolteachers when they are not guiding groups through the seething waters.

In between the rapids we got a great view of the biology of the river. As we rounded a bend Hilarie pointed out five turkey vultures roosting in a dead tree, looking like a scene from an Edgar Allan Poe mystery. "They're nature's garbage men," she said, noting that vultures, also called buzzards, clean up fish carcasses or any food scraps mistakenly left by rafters or picnickers.

You can tell a turkey vulture in flight from a hawk or an eagle, she said, by the way it holds its wings. A vulture flies with its wing tips slightly raised to form a V shape; an eagle or a hawk flies with its wings outstretched horizontally. Both can be distinguished from an osprey, which has a smaller body and white underparts.

A vulture in the air finds an upward moving air mass to take it aloft, then glides effortlessly downward in its search for prey. In calm air the vulture can stay aloft with little effort by manipulating the size of the slots in its broad wings, the position of its feather tips, and the angle of its wings. In rough air, however, it rocks unsteadily, looking as though it might literally fall out of the sky.

A turkey vulture has a wing span of nearly six feet and is black with a naked red head. Because the vulture lacks grasping talons, it cannot catch its prey in midair as do other raptors but must feed instead on animals that are already dead. It uses its sense of smell as well as its sharp eyes to find food. Even a well-hidden carcass will attract a vulture if it is odoriferous enough.

The gas released by the decaying meat stimulates the vulture and leads it to the food source.

Paulownia Tree

The New River is one of the few rivers in North America that flows from south to north as it connects the eastern coastal plains with the Midwest and the Mississippi Valley. In the course of playing this geographical role, the river carries seeds from one region to another. In the New River Gorge, as a result, you will find not only plants common to the North but many common to the South and even the West. More than a thousand plant species, biologists say, grow at this geographical crossroads. Ranger Bill Hoffmeyer guided us around the gorge (on foot this time) so we could behold this amazing diversity.

Bill showed us evidence of how the northward flow of the river has carried countless spores and seeds from the southern Appalachians into West Virginia. Among the southern plants that have migrated into the gorge are the Catawba rhododendron, whose magenta flowers paint the mountainsides in May, and the Carolina silverbell, a deciduous tree common far to the South. He pointed across the river where coniferous pines and hemlocks, usually found in the South, intruded into a forest of deciduous hardwoods common to the North.

An even stranger import, Bill told us, is the paulownia tree, a species that has long been considered worthless in the United States but is highly prized in Asian countries such as Japan.

This small tree, a species exotic to West Virginia, got its start in the gorge when railroad freight shippers discarded seed pods of the Asian plant that had been used as filler material to cushion fragile cargoes such as porcelain from China (where the paulownia is known as the "empress"). When the cargo was unpacked, the seed pods fell on favorable ground or were carried along by the river and distributed throughout the valley. Today the paulownia, with its large waxy leaves shaped like elephant ears, displays its fragrant, trumpet-shaped lavender blooms each May, particularly along the railroad tracks that parallel the river through the gorge.

Foresters in this country consider the paulownia almost a weed because it grows at the rate of about ten feet a year. But not so in Japan where a good-size tree trunk is worth one thousand

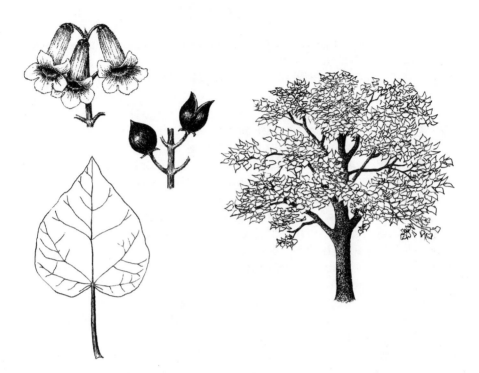

paulownia

dollars and its blond, balsalike wood is used to make coffins, kimono closets, cabinets, and musical instruments. A Japanese father traditionally plants a paulownia tree when a baby girl is born; years later he will cut the full-grown tree and fashion it into a bridal chest for his daughter when she marries.

When the supply of paulownia dwindled some years ago in Japan, the pent-up demand generated imports from other countries. At New River law enforcement rangers stay alert for tree rustlers with an eye on export who trespass in the river park to illegally cut and steal paulownia trees that sometimes grow to fifty feet in height.

Butterflies

Butterflies, common along New River during the summer, flitted around us. Butterflies, Bill said, live in a wide variety of habitats, some damp and some dry, along rivers or lakes or in high meadows.

A dozen butterflies with iridescent wings that were blue on top and black with orange spots underneath lighted atop a nearby bush that had a conical cap of flowers. "That's the spicebush swallowtail," Bill said. "It sucks the nectar from the tall, fragrant flowers of the spicebush." The spicebush, he added, thrives in a moist environment, often growing as it did here under a canopy of taller deciduous trees along the edge of a river or stream. It is often called the forsythia of the wild because of its yellow blossom, which adds the first touch of color to riverbank vegetation when the bush blooms in March or April.

The spicebush swallowtail spends its entire life around its host bush, raising two broods each year. In early summer you may open a spicebush leaf to find in its fold the silk webbing spun by the butterfly to protect its larvae. Check the same leaf several weeks later and you may see the mature caterpillar—a brilliant green with two large black and yellow spots on its back just behind the head. From the caterpillar will develop the colorful butterfly.

You can learn to identify other butterflies, Bill remarked, by noting the bush or flower they use as a food source. The silver-and-black striped zebra swallowtail, for example, is almost always found near the small understory tree, the pawpaw, because its caterpillar thrives on the foliage of this tree. Look for the buckeye butterfly feeding on thistles that grow along roadsides. The familiar monarch butterfly gets its nectar from the milkweed plant, incorporating certain toxins from the milkweed into its body that make the monarch an ill-tasting meal for a potential predator.

Bill also gave us three tips on how to distinguish a butterfly from a moth. When at rest, he said, a butterfly holds its wings vertically over its back whereas a moth spreads its wings in a horizontal position. Butterflies forage during the day, but moths are most active at night. And the antennas of butterflies usually end in a small knob while moth antennas are feathery.

Bill led the way to a place where the river flowed shallowly over flat rocks. He showed us mussel shells six inches across, tiny Asiatic shells, and small crayfish. A green-and-red plant called coon hair waved its fronds in the shallow water. We picked our way carefully across the slippery surface of sandstone and conglomerate rocks. We found that we kept our footing best in places where the water was actively flowing; the slipperiest spots were where water had gathered in a pocket, allowing algae and plant life to grow.

At length our walk across the flats brought us to the lip of Sandstone Falls. We stood watching as tons of water thundered over the ledge. It reminded us that here we were seeing the cutting edge of the gorge. The river, as it had for millions of years, was carving its way through the canyon. As visitors to New River, we felt privileged to witness the age-old process of a mighty river still hard at work.

Ecology of a Gorge

We learned about the natural history of another gorge in the Finger Lakes region of New York State. Walking the trails of Taughannock Falls State Park, we thrilled to its 215-foot waterfall (higher than Niagara Falls) and observed some of the vegetation that grows in moist gorges that have been cut into the bedrock by glacial meltwater.

A gorge like Taughannock, we discovered, has an ecosystem all its own. Just as you encounter various life zones as you climb a mountain, so also do you pass through different life zones as you descend into a gorge. On the rim grow trees typical of a forest of the middle Appalachian Mountains: white, red, and pitch pine; red, white, and chestnut oak; and shagbark hickory. At the bottom of the gorge, where temperatures grow cooler, the air is moister, and the soil is richer from erosion of the steep banks, you find trees such as sugar maple, basswood, beech, and black birch. The black birch was once the source of birch beer and the popular wintergreen flavor used in candies and medicine.

Sycamore, willow, black locust, and cottonwood thrive in the damp soil along the stream bank. Sycamores, whose bark looks like a living brown-and-white jigsaw puzzle, can grow to be six hundred years old. The Indians once used their hollow trunks to make dugout canoes.

Vegetation on the steep gorge walls depends in large part on how much sunlight the plants get and on other factors like soil composition, moisture, and temperature. On a north-facing slope

How Rangers Sample Water Quality

Knowing that pollution once almost eliminated the shad from the river, rangers at Delaware Water Gap continually check the water's quality. Seasonal Ranger Jenifer Rituper explained how water quality tests are performed. She got our group's attention with some startling facts: 70 percent of the earth's surface is water and 70 percent of each human body is made up of water. Only about 1 percent of the earth's vast store of water, however, is available for man to use — the remainder is in the oceans or locked within the earth where we cannot easily get at it.

She asked two boys to wade to the center of Dingman's Creek, a tributary of the Delaware, and fill a test tube with clear water. Following Jenifer's instructions, they put several drops of a chemical into the test tube, then compared the resulting color with a chart to determine the pH rating of the stream (its degree of acidity). Acidity is judged on a scale of 14: the lower the number the more acid the stream. For example, Jenifer said, a strong acid like battery acid will measure 1.0 n the scale, while a strong alkali such as lye will measure 13.0. Normal rainfall usually measures about 6.0, slightly acidic, because the rain interacts with carbon dioxide in the air as it falls. The water sample the boys had collected registered a healthy 7.0, or neutral, which meant the creek was evenly balanced between acidic and alkaline.

As a stream grows more and more acidic, Jenifer told the group, one species of life after another disappears. Some aquatic creatures are more tolerant of acid conditions than others. Clams, minnows, and snails, for example, need water that is only lightly acidic (6.5) to survive, but the wood frog can live in water quite a bit more acidic (4.5). A brook trout where it is normally shady, for example, eastern hemlock, yellow birch, and American yew grow. Not only can these trees and shrubs tolerate the lack of sunlight, they have tenacious root systems that can get a good grip on the steep banks. On a south-facing slope, red cedar, oaks, and hickories flourish in the warmer, sun-

can live in water with a pH level of 5.0 while its cousin the rainbow trout will survive only at the less acidic 6.0 level.

The boys took another stream sample, this time to determine the amount of dissolved oxygen in the water. The result was 11 parts per million, better than the 8 parts per million that is the minimum to support fish and amphibians. Dingman's Creek has obviously absorbed a plentiful supply of oxygen. Next, a girl waded to center stream to take the water temperature. The amount of dissolved oxygen in the water, Jenifer explained, together with the water's temperature, tells how much oxygen is being produced by the plant life of a stream.

Finally, Jenifer instructed the children to sample the stream for macroinvertebrates, the tiny organisms that live in the watercourse. Picking up a flat rock, she gently scraped several tiny creatures into a plastic tub. She also emptied into the tub the contents of a dip net a girl had swept through the shallows. An inch-long stonefly nymph crawled along the bottom of the tub, its feelers twitching back and forth. A mayfly nymph appeared with the wings it would need when it emerged from the water. Jenifer dipped her hand into the tub and produced a caddisfly larva, a soft-bodied insect that protects itself inside a cylinder of small sand grains it cements together with mucous. It lives inside this little fortress, carrying it along wherever it goes. In the stream the caddisfly lives by spinning its own net to collect the tiny organisms on which it feeds.

When the experiment was over, Jenifer asked her audience what they had learned. They summarized their results: the pH content of the water in Dingman's Creek was good, it had plenty of dissolved oxygen, and it supported a variety of creatures that found the stream a good place to live. Conclusion: on this day Dingman's Creek was a very healthy stream.

nier, and drier conditions. On the valley floor the soil may be more neutral than the soil along the rim because lime leaches out of the soil at the rim, dissolves in the rainwater, and trickles down into the valley.

The plants in a gorge support the animal life you find there. As we walked the trails we occasionally turned over a rock to find underneath a newt or a red-backed salamander. The brightly colored red-back is an amphibian that is born in the water but lives most of its life on land. It has tiny eyes but a keen sense of smell that enables it to sense its environment. It uses its long sticky tongue to snare insects or worms. Since it likes dark, moist places, you should look for salamanders in rotting stumps, depressions, or rock crevices as well as under rocks and logs.

Along the stream bank we found frogs and toads trying to stay out of sight in the dense vegetation of ferns and grasses. Although they belong to the same biological class, frogs differ from toads in several ways. Frogs live most of their life in water and dive for protection; toads live on land, going to the water only to breed. A frog possesses a smooth, moist skin while a toad has a broader, flatter body and darker, drier skin that is usually covered with warts.

For certain birds, too, a gorge provides just the right environment. A rough-winged swallow sweeps above the stream, intent on snagging in midair one of a variety of insects that incubate in the stream. The rough-wing nests in crevices in the steep walls of the gorge. The slate-colored junco also calls the gorge home, as does the gray-brown phoebe that flies and twists in the air like a miniature daredevil pilot doing a barrel roll. You can spot a phoebe by watching the bird twitch its tail up and down when it lands and by listening for its call, which sounds like its name: FEE-be, FEE-be.

Tony Ingraham, the conservation educator for the parks in the Finger Lakes region, told us of another bird you might find at Taughannock Gorge: the Louisiana water thrush. With its brownish wings and striped white breast, it looks like its cousin, the northern waterthrush. It is a surprise to find this southern native in New York State, Tony said, but it is at the northernmost part of its range. The bird, he added, is actually not a thrush but a warbler; it has a melodious call that features three clear whistles. It eats crustaceans and insects it finds by pecking along the stream.

Few mammals make their home in a closed-in gorge like Taughannock, Tony said, because the habitat does not provide what they need and their escape routes are limited. But even without mammals, gorges abound with fascinating species of wildlife.

LAKES

The natural bowls that are cradled between the slopes of the Appalachians hold hundreds of lakes; here boaters launch canoes and outboards and anglers pull fish from the water. Lake resorts such as those in the Adirondacks and Poconos stay open year round, offering vacation packages for the whole family: boating and backpacking in the summer, skiing and snowmobiling in the winter.

A group of lakes in the rolling hills of central New York State gave us a perspective on lake wildlife. The Finger Lakes serve as the heart of a busy recreation vacationland. The six major and five smaller lakes are long and slender like the fingers of a giant hand. As we toured their edges we learned about their geological origins.

Enormous sheets of ice, the last one melting only some ten thousand years ago, pushed their way south from Canada. The huge glaciers, some as much as a mile thick, gouged deep depressions in stream valleys that already existed, pushing mounds of rock and debris ahead of them like giant snowplows. When the ice melted, the water filled these depressions. The southern tips of the lakes mark the farthest point in the advance of the glaciers. Here the icy juggernauts deposited heaps of rocks and gravel, which geologists call terminal, or recessional, moraines.

Migrating Birds

At the northern end of fifty-mile-long Cayuga Lake, one of the Finger Lakes, the lake grows shallow; there a watery wetland supports the nesting and migration needs of thousands of geese, ducks, and other waterfowl.

In the early 1900s this stopover spot for waterfowl was almost lost. Construction of the Erie Canal and a connecting canal to the Finger Lakes drained much of the wetland. In 1937, howev-

A moist environment greets you at Watkins Glen State Park in the Finger Lakes region of New York. Visitors stroll behind a lacy cascade that continues to alter the shape of this deep chasm. Ferns, columbine, and hemlocks clothe the steep slopes, thriving in the dampness.

er, the U. S. Fish and Wildlife Service established Montezuma National Wildlife Refuge. Purchasing 6,432 acres of dried-up marshland, the Service built a series of dikes to impound water that flows into the area.

"The refuge lies at an important crossroads on the Atlantic flyway," Outdoor Recreation Planner Kim Johnson told us when we visited the wetland. "We provide a sort of resting and refueling stop for the birds, many of which travel hundreds of miles on their natural migration routes."

The noisiest and most visible of these fly-in visitors are the Canada geese that populate the refuge in April and May on their way north to their Hudson Bay breeding grounds, and in October on their way south to the Carolinas. In the spring, Kim said, the marshes are dotted with as many as 140,000 birds at a time; the peak fall population has reached 150,000.

If you come to the refuge at these times of year to see the geese, try to arrive either early in the morning or in the early evening, she advised. In the morning the birds head out over the countryside to spend the day feeding on grain, grass sprouts, and aquatic vegetation in fields or ponds. In the evening, as the sun sets and dusk falls, they return to their roosting place.

Canada geese may be the most numerous species to come to Montezuma, but they are not even close to being the long-distance migration champions. That distinction belongs to the white-rumped sandpiper, which starts its migration journey in Canada's Northwest Territories and flies through Montezuma to the Caribbean and all the way to Uruguay in South America. Other long-distance fliers are the blue-winged teal, which travels from Manitoba to the West Indies, and the ruby-throated hummingbird, which flies from Canada's Maritime Provinces to Central America.

Osprey

The osprey, another long-distance traveler that migrates to Peru and Brazil in the winter, makes the refuge its home in the summer. One day while scanning the watery horizon with her binoculars from the raised observation deck at the visitor center, Marge spotted a large bird standing on a nest atop a pole. It was barely visible above the waving sea of marsh grass.

A sign tipped us off that if we went to a higher level of the observation deck we could use a telescope that was trained on the osprey's nest. To our delight, when we took a look through the high-powered scope we saw not one but two ospreys, a male and a female, standing atop the collection of sticks. Beneath them a baby osprey poked its head out of the nest looking for a snack.

Marva Smith, a summer intern at the refuge, told us that refuge personnel had built the platform for the ospreys—far enough from the visitor center to maintain osprey privacy but

osprey

close enough so visitors could watch the big birds. The ospreys cooperated. They shifted their nest from a nearby location to the handy platform, mated, and reared their offspring. "We've made daily observations of the osprey family," Marva said. "Once the egg hatch, the female stays at the nest to guard it while the male flies off to get food."

The osprey is called a fish hawk for good reason. The bird wheels and soars over lakes, rivers, bays, and the ocean until it spies the fish it seeks, then plunges downward into the water and grasps the fish in its talons. In flight the osprey is smaller and slimmer than an eagle. You can recognize it by its white underside, the large black spot under each wing, and the characteristic bend at the "elbow" of the wing that sweeps the wingtips backward.

Ospreys, Marva reported, are attentive to their young and mate for life. The male flies back to the nest with its catch, but it is the female that determines the proper bite size and feeds the offspring. Both of the parents, we noticed, protected the newly hatched fledgling by stretching out their broad wings to shield it from the bright sun.

Now that one osprey has hatched and fledged at this site, Marva said, it is likely the family will return to the same nest in future years, hopefully to raise another baby osprey. That's good news for wildlife watchers.

Purple Loosestrife

To see the rest of the refuge, we drove the four-mile auto tour road on an elevated roadway that gives you a close-up look at marsh life. We watched red-winged blackbirds flitting through the sea of grass, alighting perilously on the swaying tip of a cattail. The gray of the water and the green of the swamp grass were punctuated by splashes of color from wildflowers.

One such flower was purple loosestrife, an aggressive, exotic plant that has found a perfect home for itself along the water's edge. This import from Eurasia is pretty to look at but a problem for resource managers. It grows on slender stems two to three feet high with its lavender flowers arranged vertically along the stem. A vigorous plant, it grows rapidly and expands its range relentlessly, taking over areas formerly occupied by native plants such as cattails, sedges, and rushes. In a few years a diverse wetland that used to harbor a variety of plant and wildlife species can become a single mass of purple that supports little life beyond itself. Such a loss of native food means that wetland wildlife such as ducks, grebes, muskrats, and beavers have to forage elsewhere.

CHAPTER
4

Southern Mountains and Lowlands

RIVERS

In the southeastern part of the country many rivers begin life in the highlands that mark the southern end of the Appalachian Mountains, then flow across the piedmont and coastal plain to reach the Atlantic Ocean. Moving along rapidly at first, they flow downhill through forested slopes of slash, long-leaf, and loblolly pine, slowing as they wind their way across the rolling piedmont.

As in the North, these rivers pour over the drop in elevation called the fall line that in this region encouraged the growth of such cities as Richmond, Raleigh, Columbia, and Macon.

Rivers like the Pee Dee, Broad, Savannah, and St. John slow further as they reach the coastal plain, the flattened region that sweeps in a great arc down the Atlantic coast, then curves westward along the Gulf of Mexico through Alabama, Mississippi, Louisiana, and Texas. Some rivers meander through marshlands and swamps, flowing between banks of high grass that spur the growth of aquatic life in the streams. Others snake their way across treeless, grassless areas called savannas to reach the ocean or the gulf at a broad estuary.

High temperatures, ample rainfall, a sandy soil, and a long growing season characterize the region. Marsh-loving animals such as beavers, opossums, and raccoons thrive in the watery environment as do amphibians, fish-eating birds, and a record number of snakes.

In Florida, a low-lying peninsula that geologically speaking emerged from the sea only in recent times, much of the land lies less than twenty feet above sea level. There are numerous sinkholes where rivers disappear into the ground and reappear as springs. Florida has more springs than any other state—some three hundred. Silver Springs, one of the largest, has a daily flow of half a billion gallons of water that percolates through the underlying porous limestone. The water from the springs is usually clear and clean due to the filtering action of this underground limestone labyrinth.

To the west of Florida, in the region both to the east and west of the Mississippi River, many rivers drain into the Gulf of Mexico. The Ouachita, Red, Trinity, and others get their impetus from the Ozark Plateau, a mountainous area that lies in midcontinent between the southern end of the Appalachians and the Rocky Mountains.

Limestone Geology

We became better acquainted with the Ozark Plateau as we explored the Buffalo River in Arkansas, the first river in the country to be officially designated as a national river.

As we canoed the river we learned a great deal about its limestone geology. The geologists's term for the terrain is *karst topography*. It is made up of land features formed from the limestone, which evolved from sediments laid down many years ago as an ancient sea bed. In porous terrain such as this, rainfall disappears quickly as it runs into sinkholes and other underground openings, passages, and caverns. Underground water, which is usually slightly acidic, dissolves the soluble limestone over millions of years, creating a honeycomb of hollow places underground. Sinkholes come about when the underlying bedrock dissolves and collapses, leaving a hole in the ground surface.

The Buffalo River cuts through this limestone terrain. Its visual trademark is the high bluffs that embrace each turn in the river. The bluffs are streaked with vertical black markings where rainfall has dissolved minerals in the rocks and has run down the rock face, causing the discoloration.

At Pebble Spring, a placid pool beneath a bluff, we saw an example of karst topography. The pool was filled with hundreds of small stones, most of them smoothed into an oval shape. These stones, we learned, had taken on their smooth shape after years of

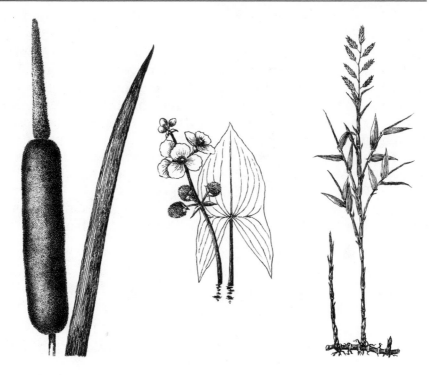

cattail, arrowhead, and river cane

rolling and bouncing as they were pushed along by the force of an underground stream. Finally, as the stream flowed to the surface the stones were ejected to become part of Pebble Spring. Here was yet another manifestation of the limestone underpinnings of this region where the rivers run not only above the ground but beneath it as well.

The river, park rangers told us, rises as much as twenty-five feet during spring floods. We saw the evidence: clumps of grass that had been caught in the notch of a tree or on a jutting fragment of the cliff some twenty feet or more above the water level and left there as a reminder of the flooding waters.

When the river level rises, animals that live along it employ a variety of strategies to survive. A beaver, for example, may be able to stay high and dry in its riverbank burrow. The raccoon carries out a different plan—it shifts to an alternate den. Each raccoon builds a number of dens within its territory. One den may be located several feet up a tree in a hollow of the trunk; others may be in a rock crevice, an overturned tree, an abandoned burrow, or a muskrat's house. When the water rises, the raccoon simply retreats to its den in the tree hollow where it is safe above the flooding river.

River Cane

Spring flooding also erodes the riverbank. A plant that is common along the Buffalo River, as well as at many other rivers, helps prevent such erosion. It is river cane.

This light green, stalky plant grows in patches close to the river. Each of its long, bamboolike stems holds up a handful of thin leaves and grows as high as eight feet. Its root system consists of rhizomes that hold the cane securely in the earth. River cane spreads as these rhizomes grow outward and multiply. As the cane spreads, the patch grows larger and the rhizomes anchor the soil to prevent it from washing away.

River cane is an edible plant. You can pick young shoots and prepare them as you would bamboo shoots. Its seeds may be ground into a flour and used as cereal.

Purple Lobelia

A three-mile trail led us along the river's banks and bluffs. Riverbanks provide an ideal habitat for many plant species. For example, in the Buffalo River corridor rangers have identified more than fifteen hundred varieties of plants. One of these is purple lobelia, a late-blooming wildflower that dotted the trail sides on this October day. Since the lobelia likes moist soil, a river valley setting suits it well.

We noticed several bees darting from one of its spiky, purplish blue flowers to their nest; we later learned that blue and purple seem to be the most fetching colors for bees, so nature has arranged that many flowers of these colors are adapted for bee pollination. The lobelia's beauty masks another interesting characteristic as well: the plant possesses a narcotic quality that can daze an animal that eats its leaves.

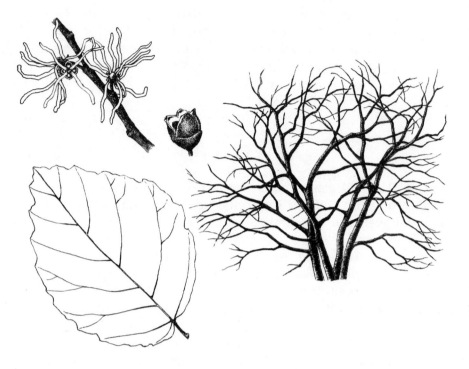

witch hazel

Witch Hazel

Witch hazel bushes were also in bloom along the trail. Their yellow flowers appear, oddly enough, after the leaves have died.
The fruits that follow do not ripen until the next growing season;
when they are ripe, the fruit pods burst open and shoot the
seeds fifteen or twenty feet away. Early Europeans, when they
discovered the seed pod's surprising ability, considered it magic
or witchery, hence the plant's name.

You can recognize this small shrub or tree (usually about six
to ten feet tall) by its oval leaves with scalloped edges and by its
jointed, curving branches that twist and point in all directions.

Witch hazel usually grows in sparse colonies of plants in the understory of moist woods. An extract of the witch hazel is used commercially in toilet water, shaving lotion, and cosmetics and its bark and leaves are used in medicines. The fruit is eaten by grouse and turkeys and its bark by squirrels and rabbits.

In earlier days, and even today, people have used forked witch hazel branches to try to find underground water through well witching, or water dowsing. Before they dig a well, some people hire a dowser, an individual believed to possess the ability to discover water. The dowser cuts a forked stick from a witch hazel bush, holds a prong in each hand with the main limb pointing ahead of him, then walks over the area where the well is needed. In theory, the end of the stick should bob violently toward the ground if underground water exists close to the surface at that spot. Experienced dowsers are even said to be able to predict how many feet deep the well should be and whether the water is pure enough to drink. A ranger told us later that although some people refuse to believe in the scientific validity of well witching, many of the good wells in the Ozarks were located by this method.

Sumac

Sumac, a shrub or small tree that grows to the height of a person, has an easily recognized compound leaf with thin leaflets. It produces clusters of hairy red fruit that hang at the end of its branches like a bunch of grapes. Historians believe the Indians chewed the roots of the smooth sumac to rid themselves of mouth sores and mashed its leaves and fruits into a paste to treat poison ivy rash.

Keep your eye out, however, for another variety of sumac— the poison sumac. You can distinguish it from the harmless members of its family by its longer and more pointed compound leaves and its white rather than reddish brown fruits. Another clue is that the poison sumac is almost always found in a swamp. Touching this plant can give you a serious skin irritation with inflammation, itching, and blistering. Oddly enough, however, birds love the poison sumac. It serves as a valuable source of winter food for songbirds and game birds because the fruits remain on the plants when other food is scarce.

Sassafras

Sassafras, a medium-sized tree of the laurel family, is easily identified by the fragrance and taste of its green twigs, leaves, and
bark. The sassafras grows as high as eighty feet with a trunk up
to six feet thick. It has slender branches and leaves that have an
irregular shape and smooth edges—often shaped like a mitten.
Its bark, when young, is reddish brown and divided by shallow
fissures. Sassafras leafs out late in the spring; once the buds
burst, the heavy glossy leaves form rapidly.

You can follow an Indian tradition with sassafras if you
desire and dig up its roots, wash them, cut them into pieces, and
boil them in water to make a pleasant-tasting tea. Sassafras
played an interesting role in the early exploration of the country.
Many people attributed imaginary virtues to this plant, believing
it a curative because of its sweet smell and taste. English explorers who investigated the North American coast sailed back home
with their holds full of sassafras to meet the medical demand for
this tasty plant.

Wintergreen

Close to the ground grow clumps of wintergreen, a creeping plant
that reaches only a few inches high. It has shiny, oval leaves one
to two inches long, small, waxy, egg-shaped flowers that dangle
beneath its leaves, and a small red berry that has a strong wintergreen flavor. The wintergreen spreads by sending out underground runners that send up shoots as new plants. If you are
walking a riverside trail and see a patch of it, you can nibble on
its sweet-tasting leaves or fruit. (Always make a positive identification before eating any plant, however.) Oil of wintergreen has
long been used to flavor medicines and cosmetics.

Mistletoe

We also noticed clumps of green, leathery leaves growing in the
upper branches of a large sycamore. "Mistletoe," ranger Mike
Holmes identified. "It's called a parasite because it draws its moisture and nutrients from another living thing. It grows in the tops

of the tree where its tendrils root in crevices in the sycamore bark."

Birds, he said, eat its white, shiny fruits. The seeds spread and take root when a bird carrying mistletoe seeds flies to another tree to sharpen its bill against its bark.

"Could too many mistletoe plants kill a tree?" we asked. "They could," Mike said, "although these sycamores can tolerate quite a few. If a tree did die, we would leave the dead tree standing," he said, explaining the Park Service's management policy of allowing natural processes to continue unimpeded in the river corridor. "Dead trees and snags," he added, "make excellent homes for owls, raccoons, and woodpeckers."

Armadillo

As we moved quietly down the trail Marge heard a rustle in some leaves up the slope. We stopped to listen and watch, using our binoculars to focus on the location of the rustling sound. About fifty yards away some leaves moved and we saw the smooth, shiny back of an armadillo scuttling away from this intrusion into its domain. It was a thrill—the first armadillo we had seen in the wild. A ranger deflated us later by telling us that armadillos are common throughout the Ozarks.

Common or not, the armadillo has been called North America's oddest mammal. It has a scaled head like a lizard's, ears like a mule's, claws like a bear's, and a tail like a rat's. It wears a bony shell that gives it the appearance of a pint-sized gladiator. All this accounts for its name, given by the Spanish conquistadors: "little fellow in armor."

We had undoubtedly interrupted the animal as it was feeding in the moist area we were walking through. The wetter the soil, the easier it is for the armadillo to dig out the insects, worms, beetles, crickets, grasshoppers, slugs, and snails that make up most of its diet. It pokes its pointed snout into the soil or a rotting log and digs for its prey with its short, strong front legs and big claws. With one quick swipe of its tongue it can lap up a whole batch of ants, which it gobbles down whole. Its eyesight is poor, but a superb sense of smell allows it to locate insects as deep as six inches beneath the ground. It varies its diet with small fruits and seeds and drinks a good deal of water. This need for water means that when the armadillo inhabits an arid area it must stay close to a watercourse or find a natural spring.

This animal spends much of its time sleeping in its burrow, sometimes in company with another armadillo or even a cotton-tail rabbit, skunk, or mouse. Its burrow, located on a hillside or in a brush pile, extends some twenty-five feet and ends in a grass-

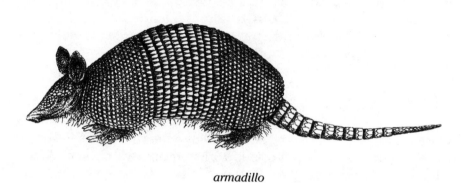

armadillo

lined chamber. Like the raccoon, the armadillo may make use of a number of burrows spread around its home range.

The armadillo has developed an ingenious way of getting across a creek. Before crossing, it gulps down a large quantity of air, which inflates its intestines and keeps it afloat as it swims across the water.

Bats

More than a hundred caves dot the terrain around the Buffalo River. Many are narrow and enclosed, potentially more treacher-ous than an open rock shelter because their eroding interiors make for difficult footing. One cave known to the rangers has seven miles of mapped passages. Rangers warn hikers not to ven-ture into such caves but to leave exploration to experienced cavers who will make their way carefully into the interior with the help of caving equipment and lights.

Many of these caves are host to several species of bats. Bats often roost in caves that are near rivers and lakes because these bodies of water provide rich environments for insect populations.

A ranger told us that, surprisingly, bats are one of the most common of mammals although you will rarely see one. In fact, one-fifth of all mammal species are bats. Bats also have the distinction of being the only mammal that can truly fly. Buffalo River bat species include the eastern pipistrelle and the big brown bat as well as several endangered species.

The reason you see bats so rarely, of course, is that they are nocturnal. When the sun goes down and the air over the river grows moister, they emerge from their damp caves to patrol back and forth over the river, flying low as they snap up insects like moths, midges, mayflies, and dragonflies.

Bats eat vast numbers of insects and are the only major predator of night-flying insects. They find their prey at night or in the utter darkness of a cave by echolocation, a technique inventors did their best to duplicate when they produced sonar, the system that enables naval vessels to detect submarines. A bat produces a twittering sound so high pitched that humans cannot hear its full range. These sound waves strike objects in their path of flight, sending back echoes to the bat's ears. The echoes tell the bat how it must turn in the air to avoid an object or find its prey. With this sensitive sound system, bats navigate skillfully despite the darkness. Using these hunting techniques, a bat can devour one-third to one-half of its weight in insects each night.

A bat roosts during the day, hanging from the ceiling of a cave by its hind feet, the wings draped around its body like a cloak. It is clumsy on the ground because its wings get in its way and its knees bend backward. But in the air few birds can fly as expertly as a bat.

Bats become even less visible during the winter when they hibernate, often from early October until the following May. They carefully choose a cave where the humidity is high enough to prevent them from becoming dehydrated over the winter. When the weather warms again in the spring, the bats emerge from their long sleep.

In the summertime when they raise their families, some species of bats gather together in large maternity colonies. The colonies usually consist of females, newborn young, and a few males. Females do not search out their own offspring; they nurse any youngster that approaches. But if a young bat falls to the cave floor, it is abandoned and soon perishes.

If you are in cave country where bats are known to live, look inside a cave during the day. You may see the bats hanging head-down from protrusions in the ceiling. Bats have weak legs—some species cannot walk at all. So they simply hang from a roost by their legs, using their semicircular pointed toes to ensure a firm grip. Another indication of the presence of bats is an accumulation of light-colored guano on the cave floor.

Several caves in the country provide a rare opportunity to see these nocturnal mammals in action. Best known is Carlsbad Caverns National Park in southeastern New Mexico, where a park naturalist explains the bat flight each evening at the cave entrance. Another is Frio Cave in central Texas, where some ten to fifteen million Mexican free-tailed bats emerge from below ground on summer evenings. As the sun goes down the bats begin to fly out in groups, forming a counterclockwise swirl that makes a loud roaring noise and a huge dark cloud visible for miles.

Fish Food Chain

The Chattahoochee River in Georgia provides a place for thousands of urban dwellers from Atlanta and elsewhere to enjoy the almost wilderness character of this river corridor. Many of the visitors choose to take a raft, canoe, or kayak float trip on the "Hooch." Those seeking a wilderness experience of a day's fishing in solitude, on the other hand, head for the upper part of the river. Only a half-hour drive north of Atlanta, a fisherman can find a deserted section of the river, a ramp to launch his boat—and a wide variety of fish to challenge his skills.

At the bottom of the food chain are members of the minnow family such as dace, shiners, stone rollers, and chubs. These small fish are preyed on by larger fish like bass, perch, muskie, and pike.

Suckers cruise along the bottom, using their underslung mouth like a vacuum cleaner to snap up larvae, worms, fish eggs, and vegetation from the bottom. Bewhiskered catfish, which feed mostly at night, prowl the riverbed with their feelers spread, ready to dive into the mud to snare a crustacean, snail, or insect larvae.

Crappies represent the sunfish family; a crappie is gray along the top of its body grading to an off-white at the bottom. A plump fish, it usually weighs about one pound and is much desired by fishermen as panfish. Crappies feed on underwater weeds, brush, or stumps. During the day they frequent deep holes; toward evening they feed in schools near the surface.

Smallmouth bass and yellow perch are other angler favorites. The smallmouth, an average of one pound in weight and olive in color, has a large dorsal fin. This fish is so sensitive to outside influences that it can even detect a person's footsteps on a nearby riverbank. Both it and the yellow perch—which, oddly enough, is gray in color—eat crayfish, insects, small fishes, and fish eggs. In the spring you might see a gelatinous rope of fish eggs as long as seven feet entwined among the water weeds. This rope holds the eggs of the yellow perch. As the eggs absorb water the rope grows to several times the adult's weight before the fry hatch out.

At the top of the fish food chain in the Chattahoochee are the muskellunge and northern pike. Both of these large, aggressive fish prey on other fish such as suckers and perch. In the early spring, a muskie will lay as many as ten thousand eggs that cling to water weeds and to the river bottom. Fry hatch in about two weeks and quickly turn killers. Consuming hundreds of forage fish such as minnows, they grow to six inches long by the end of sixty days. Adults become lone-wolf hunters, drifting motionless in the water then lunging forward to grab their prey.

The upper reaches of the river hold a fairly large trout population, although the Chattahoochee is not a natural trout stream at all. When Buford Dam, built in 1906 for hydroelectricity and flood control, releases water from its back-up reservoir Lake Lanier, the released water comes from the depths of the lake and is cold enough for trout. Georgia's fish specialists then release fingerlings of rainbow, brook, and brown trout from hatcheries into the cold water—some 140,000 fingerlings a year.

Opossum

To get an insight into the flora and fauna along the river, we visited the Chattahoochee Nature Center. Here we became acquainted with the plant communities and birds, fish, mammals, and other wildlife that live in the river corridor. The day we visited the low-lying, rustic center, Tammy Rogers of the volunteer staff was holding up an opossum to show a group of third graders who sat in a circle around her feet. The possum, she explained, has an opposable thumb like a human being that enables this unusual animal to get a firm grip on a tree branch and to more easily handle its food. She pointed out that the animal eats not only rodents, insects, and frogs but can even kill and eat a venomous snake.

Tammy related that the opossum is the only marsupial found in the United States. A marsupial is an animal that carries its young in a pouch that forms a built-in incubator on its belly. Opossums are born in groups of five to twenty. At birth an opossum is only as big as a kidney bean. The tiny newborn crawls from the birth canal into the pouch where the mother opossum carries it for about two months after birth. After leaving the pouch, the young stay near the mother for several more weeks.

The opossum is about the size of a house cat and is light gray in color with a darker band running along its back. It has a narrow head covered with white hair that tapers to a pointed snout and large, hairless ears. During the day it may be curled up in a tree cavity. After dark it descends from the safety of the branches to forage for its food on the ground.

Although the opossum looks mean with its narrow snout and fifty teeth, it is actually quite timid. Its keen sense of hearing is its best hunting weapon as it makes its nighttime patrol. Its ears twitch as it listens for any noise that will tell it the exact location of its prey.

Tammy reminded the youngsters of the term "playing possum" and explained how the phrase came about. If an opossum finds itself in danger from a predator, she said, it uses a unique defense: it feigns death, actually seeming to fall into a trance, its eyes and mouth open and its body limp. At the same time, it exudes a smell that is distasteful to other animals. If the would-be predator is confused and departs, the opossum quickly arouses and goes on its way.

Cattail

When we left the center we walked a boardwalk trail that wound along the river's edge. The trail led through the different types of marsh environment: the standing water of a pond; the cattail community where cattails thrive in the shallows; the sedge and grass community that grows in the drier marshland; and the driest community of all, the swampland where alder and willow grow.

A clump of cattails nodded their brown cylindrical heads in the breeze. The heads are actually the plant's closely packed blossoms that are fertilized by pollen from the spikelike male flowers that grow at the tip of each branch.

This familiar marsh plant grows up to nine feet high and often forms extensive stands. Its leaves have swordlike, sharp edges and grow from a stiff unbranched stem that is topped by the sausage-shaped heads. The heads are green in the springtime and turn brown in the fall. In the late winter the head tears apart, scattering the fluff-topped seeds.

The cattail is one of the most versatile and edible plants you will find around rivers and lakes. You can gather and eat the young flowers in the spring, as the colonial settlers learned from the Indians. Early in the plant's growing season you can cook and eat the shoots that sprout from its roots—they taste like crunchy asparagus. Muskrats and geese, too, like the cattail; they feed on its underwater roots. Red-winged blackbirds and other birds find a stand of cattails good protective cover, and teals eat its tiny seeds.

Jewelweed

A sign alongside the boardwalk identified jewelweed, a plant that thrives in wetlands. Jewelweed grows three to five feet in height on a translucent stalk. Also called touch-me-not, it has an oval-shaped leaf and a pale orange-yellow blossom. If you touch one of its ripe pods in the summer, the pod will spring open with a snap, flinging its seeds in all directions. Jewelweed is said to be an antidote to poison ivy and often grows near it; simply break off several leaves or part of the stalk and rub their juices against the exposed area to ease the itching.

Arrowhead

The arrowhead plant takes root below the water level and grows about two feet above water. Widespread in marshy areas of the country, this plant has an arrow-shaped leaf the size of your hand and a white flower with a yellow center that blooms in mid-summer.

Perhaps the best thing about arrowhead for wildlife is the edible tuber or bulb that grows from its roots. Ducks pull off these two-inch tubers to eat, accounting for one of the plant's nicknames, "duck potatoes." You might try them too. Botanists say they are nutritious, sweet in flavor, and safe to eat. You may roast, bake, boil, or cream them—or serve them like french fries!

Ecology of a Swamp Forest

The slow-motion Congaree River forms an even more watery environment than a marsh. Conforming to the terrain of South Carolina's "Midlands," the Congaree twists like a brownish snake across the flatland toward the Atlantic Ocean.

Robert McDaniel, superintendent of Congaree Swamp National Monument, told us about this unique river in a small visitor center tucked deep in the rural Carolina landscape. "When heavy rains fill the creeks and rivers of this drainage basin, the Congaree cannot hold all the water from these upstream tributaries within its banks. So the water overflows onto the broad, flat floodplain you see around here—often ten or twelve times a year."

This periodic flooding, he explained, produces several effects. The force of the surging water can change the landscape. On several occasions floodwaters have straightened a bend in the river, carving a shortcut. The former river bend is left behind as an oxbow lake when the river takes a new course.

The floodwaters also carry tons of silt from upstream into the Congaree Swamp. As the brown deluge spreads over these lowlands it deposits nutrients that keep the swamp a fertile growing area. The result of this natural fertilization from upstream is a river-bottom hardwood forest that nourishes some of the oldest and largest trees on the Atlantic seaboard.

"This fifteen thousand-acre park is one of the few areas in the South that has not been cut over by the timber companies," Bob said, "so these trees have continued to add to their growth.

Some are more than a century old. The oldest tree we know of within the park is a bald cypress that is six hundred years old. We also preserve more than twenty trees that are of near-record or state-record size. We estimate we have about 160 trees that are more than ten feet in circumference."

The superintendent recommended two ways to explore this swampy forest, and neither of these is by car. "Most of our roads skirt the boundaries," he said, "so the best way to see the real swamp is by canoe or on foot." For those who prefer the on-foot option an elevated boardwalk permits visitors to walk above the swampy terrain from the visitor center into the heart of the wetland at Weston Lake, an oxbow in the river before it was isolated when the Congaree changed its channel.

Rain fell gently the gray morning we walked the three-and-a-half-mile trail with Park Naturalist Fran Rametta. In the mist the glistening trees and vegetation surrounding us gave the scene an otherworldly appearance.

The boardwalk starts at the higher fringe of the swamp, the area least often flooded. Here the prominent tall trees are the sweet gum, southern hackberry, southern red oak, swamp white oak, overcup oak, several species of hickory, cottonwood, black gum, and sycamore. Less common are beech, white ash, and several species of elm.

Below the big trees grows an understory of red maple, American holly, red mulberry, and dogwood. Shrubs fill in the gaps: blue beech, pawpaw, strawberry bush, planer tree, spicebush, and dwarf palmetto—the variety of vegetation is a botanist's dream.

Fran kept up a running commentary, pointing out the wonders of the rich forest. "Up there in that beech tree, see the row of holes? Yellow-bellied sapsucker," he said. "It drills a series of holes in a row and eats the sap that oozes out of them." To one side a gray tree frog sat immobile on a branch, barely distinguishable from the bark. A vine as thick as your arm and covered with hairlike rootlets swung beside the boardwalk. "Poison ivy," Fran said, as we craned our necks to follow the path of the huge vine twisting up a tree. "From the size of the vine I'd say it's an old one." A large spider web, gleaming like silver in the morning light, was suspended beneath the railing, ready to trap one of the legions of mosquitoes and other insects that call the swamp home.

The boardwalk sloped slightly downward as we entered the floodplain itself. "In a swamp like this," Fran said, "a slight difference in elevation, maybe only a few feet, makes a big difference in the vegetation that grows there." For instance, down at ground level he pointed out the dog hobble or fetterbush. This low-growing shrub earned its colorful name because its strong, vinelike branches effectively prevent hunting dogs from running through it and it fetters a man as ankle chains would a prisoner. Another interesting lower-level plant is the partridge berry. Unlike most plants, he said, it takes two of its white flowers to produce a single red berry.

Loblolly Pine

The floodplain at Congaree is inundated some ten times a year as the water level rises and falls. In this environment the loblolly pine thrives, on the average the tallest of the trees in the park. The loblolly has a straight trunk, a rounded crown and few intervening branches. It has scaly bark; on a rapidly growing loblolly the bark often cracks into sections as the girth of the tree expands.

The species got its odd name from early English settlers. When the new arrivals saw this tree growing in the New World and learned of its many uses, they gave it the name of one of their favorite all-purpose foods at home: their porridge, or loblolly. They cut the tree for lumber and used its sap to distill turpentine, which in turn made its way into lamp oil, naval stores, paint, and preservatives. Today the loblolly pine is widely used for kraft paper, newsprint, and plywood.

Among the loblollies growing at Congaree, Fran told us, is the tallest one in South Carolina. It towers 145 feet, the height of a fifteen-story building, and measures fifteen feet four inches in circumference.

Water Tupelo

A quarter of a mile farther along the boardwalk brought us to Weston Lake. Around its fringe grow two other tree species that thrive with their "feet" in the water: the water tupelo and the bald cypress.

These swamp trees are easy to identify with their imposing height and enlarged, buttressed trunks that flare out at the base to give the tree support in its wet surroundings. The water tupelo has oval leaves several inches long and bears a tiny greenish white flower and dark purple fruit. Some tupelos in the Congaree Swamp grow one hundred feet high.

Sometimes the tupelo tree reveals where a river has changed its course. Tupelos that have sprouted and grown along a river's edge remain as landmarks even when the river takes a new direction.

Bald Cypress

The bald cypress, a truly remarkable tree, is actually not a true cypress but a relative of the redwood and sequoia. Like its California cousins, the bald cypress often lives to a venerable age. Some specimens, according to foresters, have been known to live for fifteen hundred years. The bald cypress is becoming increasingly rare, however, because the draining of wetlands has decreased habitat suitable for it to grow and commercial timbermen come looking for it because its wood is so resistant to decay.

A conifer, or cone-bearing tree, the bald cypress has flat, needlelike, yellow-green leaves that turn orange-brown in the fall. It is unique among southern conifers because it sheds its leaves in the winter. It grows to heights of 120 feet or more, drawing nutrients from the spongy peatlike soil beneath the water. Its buttressed trunk and its long, thick roots anchor it firmly despite its unstable footing.

You will immediately notice another curious characteristic of the tree: its "knees." These extensions of its roots protrude upward several feet above the water level and give added support to the rest of the deep root mass beneath. Some of the trees at Congaree have knees over seven feet high that provide snug dens for a variety of swamp animals.

How can a tree like the bald cypress reproduce, we wondered, when its seed cones do not fall on the soil but into the

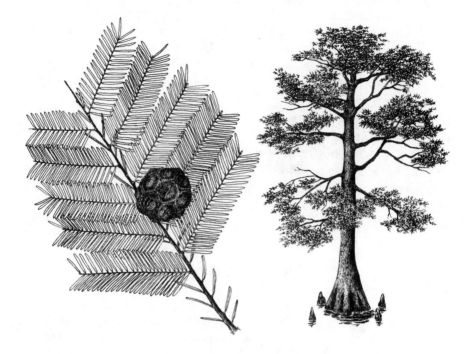

bald cypress

water? "It's not easy," Fran told us, "but every so often the water level of the swamp goes down at the same time that the seed cones drop. Then the seed cones drop on a saturated but not inundated spot and can sprout. But in order for these spouts to survive, the water level must stay down long enough for the saplings to get a start so they can withstand the next flooding." In spite of these exacting seedbed requirements, bald cypresses reproduce readily at Congaree Swamp.

We had come to the Congaree at an opportune time to appreciate the hold-fast nature of the bald cypress. Only a month before we arrived a savage hurricane had slashed across the Caribbean and the South Carolina coast. Loblolly pines had come crashing down, their shallow root systems unable to hold the trees upright against the fury of the windstorm. Yet the bald cypress trees—most of them almost as tall as the loblollies—

had come through unharmed or with only a part of their crown blown away. Their widespread root system and their network of knees had anchored them firmly against the hurricane.

Spanish Moss

In addition to our boardwalk hike we took a ranger-led canoe trip across the swamp, paddling in tea-colored water through the humid wilderness. The water's dark color comes from the tannin in decayed leaves, twigs, and debris; it is acid enough to be almost like vinegar. Huge trees arch overhead and an occasional fallen trunk makes navigation tricky.

Spanish moss, draped from overhanging tree limbs, slapped us in the face. Strangely enough, this silvery green plant is neither Spanish nor a moss. It is uniquely American and is related to the pineapple. It adorns trees from North Carolina to South America and remains one of nature's oddities.

Spanish moss is an epiphyte, a plant that has no roots but instead lives off the moisture it draws from the atmosphere. Scales of the moss's tendrils trap rain that the plant then absorbs. The scales also keep internal moisture from evaporating.

The moss gets its nourishment as rains wash nutrient-rich cells off the host tree; the greater the number of cells, the greater the moss's growth. Consequently, you will often find large masses of the moss on very old or decaying trees.

Spanish moss—also called long moss or vegetable horsehair—covers more trees than any other epiphyte. It does not bear fruit like its spiny distant cousin, the pineapple, but it sometimes produces small yellow flowers. The plant grows as long as twenty-five feet and its threadlike leaves are one to three inches long. Although Spanish moss is primarily decorative, it has been used as packing material and upholstery stuffing.

Garfish

In the dark water beneath the canoe, plump mudfish or warmouths swim, their color matching the water. A splash nearby may be garfish, that elongated, sharp-nosed denizen of the swamp that feasts on other fish. The gar often camouflages itself by lurking alongside a submerged log, which it resembles, then seizing its prey. The garfish is thin, measures from four to ten inches long, and has a tapered mouth with a lower jaw that is longer than the upper. It eats small fish or frogs, impaling them on its sharp teeth. In spite of its long, slim body it has the power to jump clear of the water to grab its prey. Garfish are also common in Florida's Everglades, where they devour fish that gather in alligator holes, and are themselves prey for the alligators.

Snakes

A brown water snake, one of many snakes that inhabit the swamp, watched us from a log. There are many different kinds of water snakes; they are the second most numerous type of snake in the country after the common garter snake. Most snakes can swim, but the water snake is more fully adapted and slithers easily through the water.

Water snakes use the water for feeding and for concealment but spend much of their time basking on the branches of overhanging trees and bushes. Some, such as the black swamp snake and striped swamp snake, emerge from the water only rarely. Instead, they stay immersed most of the time, crawling about among masses of floating water plants while foraging for crayfish and other small animals that live in the water.

Although nonpoisonous water snakes are the most numerous in the swamp, three poisonous species also inhabit the region: the cottonmouth water moccasin, canebrake or timber rattlesnake, and copperhead. You can readily distinguish any of these poisonous snakes from the nonpoisonous ones by three distinctive characteristics. First of all, the poisonous snakes are all pit vipers. Pit vipers have V-shaped, triangular heads whereas the nonpoisonous snakes have rounded heads. Secondly, pit vipers have small pit cavities located on either side of the snout between the nostril and the eye. This remarkable organ is a heat-detecting device the snake uses to sense the presence of a warm-blooded animal. Thirdly, pit vipers have vertical pupils that make their eyes look like vertical slits; nonpoisonous snakes have round pupils and round eyes.

The cottonmouth moccasin is semiaquatic and often lives along a swamp bank or in weeds where it waits to prey on fish,

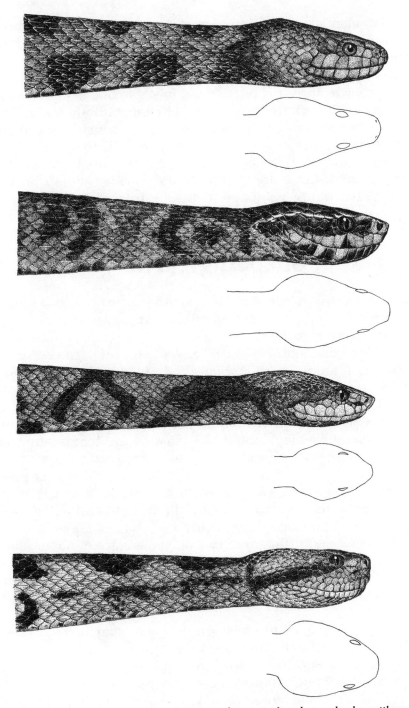

from top: brown water snake, cottonmouth, copperhead, canebrake rattlesnake

frogs, salamanders, or even other snakes. When it is disturbed, the cottonmouth's mouth gapes open, revealing a milky white interior that contrasts with the olive brown color of its body.

The canebrake rattlesnake, which gets its name from the fact that in other regions it is often found in sugarcane fields, is grayish brown with dark irregular bands circling its body and a thin rusty red stripe running along the center of its back. It prefers flight to a fight and feeds on small mammals and birds.

The copperhead is lighter in color than the other two. Its overall pinkish tan color is interspersed with reddish brown blotches of an hourglass shape. Its head is bright brown—a testimony to its name.

Snapping Turtle

As we drifted we caught sight of a snapping turtle basking on a half-submerged branch that had fallen across the water. One of the many kinds of turtles that live in muddy streams, ponds, and lakes across the country—as well as on land and in the ocean—the common snapping turtle eats fish, frogs, insects, snails, young waterfowl, and some of the plants that grow on the bottom of the swamp.

Like snakes and other reptiles, the turtle is cold-blooded: its body temperature stays about the same as the temperature of the surrounding air or water. To warm up, this snapper had stretched its limbs and head along the branch, closing its eyes against the bright sun. We noticed that its sunbathing spot was close to the water so it could easily slip from the branch if danger threatened, for example in the form of a bird of prey.

The snapping turtle grows to a maximum size of about nineteen inches and has a gray or olive-colored shell and a fairly large head. It is justifiably respected for the power of its jaws. A snapper is capable of amputating a small child's finger with a single bite.

A turtle is one of the best protected animals with its two shells, one on its back, the other beneath its belly. Most turtles can retreat fully into their shells, pulling their limbs and head in with them. A snapper, however, can only partially withdraw and relies on its fearsome bite as its second line of defense. The bony shell is the animal's skeleton. It is covered with large *scutes,* or plates of horn, that continue to grow from a layer of living skin that lies beneath the plates. Each year a new scute, or section of outer shell, appears under the previous year's layer. By counting scutes you can estimate a turtle's age, much the way you count rings to tell the age of a tree. To prove that a turtle has sensation even in its horny armor, draw your fingernail along a furrow of the shell; the turtle will react to your touch by withdrawing protectively.

When it got hungry, we knew, the basking turtle would slip into the water and settle to the bottom, there to wait until it could ambush a small fish or crayfish moving by. In order to stay underwater for a prolonged period of time, turtles have a unique way of taking oxygen from the water. In addition to breathing through a set of lungs, freshwater turtles can use their mouth cavity in gill-like fashion. Water is drawn through the nostrils, oxygen is absorbed by special organs in the mouth cavity, and the water is expelled. A few turtles can even absorb small amounts of oxygen through their skin during hibernation. As a result, many freshwater turtles have the ability to remain submerged or buried in the bottom mud for weeks at a time.

Great Blue Heron

The fish in the water attract a variety of birds. One of these, the great blue heron, was a resident of many of the rivers we visited. It has blue-gray plumage on its back and wings that shades to a whitish color on the neck. On its white head it wears black crown patches and head plumes.

The heron is a patient hunter. As it stalks the shoreline waiting for prey to venture close it lifts one foot at a time from the shallows without making a ripple, alert for any movement beneath the water. It will stand motionless for half an hour at a time until a victim comes by. Once in a while the big heron will venture into deep water, jabbing time and again with its sharp, narrow bill at a passing school of fish.

The great blue heron prefers fish but also goes after frogs, snakes, crustaceans, birds, small mammals, and insects. If given an opportunity, the blue heron will plunder a fish hatchery;

hatchery officials told us they had to keep netting over most of their breeding ponds to prevent the herons from swooping in for a free feast.

The great blue is the most widely distributed of all the herons. Look for it in coastal marshes and along rivers and lakes throughout the United States and parts of Canada. Migrating herons gather at their breeding grounds in early spring. Often they choose a secluded island or a patch of woods to carry out their elaborate courtship ritual. The male birds strut about, using their long bills like swords to prove their prowess over their rivals. Croaking females urge them on. Sometimes a group of herons dances in a circle, their large wings flapping up and down. A mating pair nibbles each other's feathers.

Herons usually build their nests in the highest treetops available, although they may occasionally use shrubs or even the ground. If you have a chance to watch you will notice that the male gathers sticks for the nest while the female arranges them in place. A new nest may be small and flimsy, but a nest that the birds are using for the second or third time will have grown to a much larger size. To spot a nest, look for a jumble of sticks atop a sturdy bush or thicket, sometimes several feet off the ground. Whitewashed excretions on branches and the ground may give you a clue that a heron's nest is high above.

High in these nests in the springtime you might see the two herons guarding their nest. The male and female take turns incubating four greenish blue eggs. Both provide food for the noisy hatchlings and at least one remains on duty at the nest at all times to guard against marauding hawks or owls.

Kingfisher

The belted kingfisher, sporting a jaunty crest on its head, flies across an open swamp area, then dives headfirst into the water, successfully grabbing a small fish in its bill. Then it flies to a branch to gobble down its prize.

The bird is from eleven to fourteen inches long; its upper parts and wings are deep blue with white markings. The underparts are white and there is a broad collar of white around the neck. The kingfisher may sit for hours on a branch beside a river or swamp waiting for a small fish to swim near it on the surface.

This waterside bird also eats crayfish, frogs, tadpoles, salamanders, and insects.

Rangers who have watched kingfishers report their interesting courtship and nesting habits. When a male and a female kingfisher first meet in the spring, the male presents the female with a fish. As he offers this prize, he holds the fish with its head outward so that the female can take it and gobble it headfirst. Young kingfishers are fed by their parents in the same way.

The pair then sets about building a nest: a hole in the stream or swamp bank that requires a good deal of bird engineering skill. First the kingfishers peck away the dirt at the selected spot to start the hole, then work their way into the growing tunnel, shoveling out earth with their feet. The tunnel has a slightly upward slope and may be a yard in length before it ends in a nest chamber.

Here the female lays her eggs. After they hatch, both father and mother help with the feeding until the small birds learn to fly and catch fish by themselves. A young kingfisher must make many more dives than an adult before it learns how to snag a fish. If the weather continues to be cold, a young kingfisher may die from this repeated wetting of its plumage.

Mississippi Kite

If you are a lucky bird-watcher you might even spot a Mississippi kite, a bird rarely seen. This falcon-sized bird has a slate gray body with lighter gray on its head and underparts. Its tail and wingtips are black.

The aerial performances of this bird are dazzling: It soars in great circles, sweeps, or dashes with vigor and grace as it sweeps the area for prey such as lizards, small snakes, frogs, grasshoppers, or beetles. It aims particularly for a large beetle of the cicada family that it can deftly pick from a tree branch as it swoops by. Like other kites, it gobbles its food on the wing. Other birds to look for in a southern swamp include woodpeckers, red-shouldered hawks, cardinals, and pine warblers.

LAKES

A lake area in the mid-South that offers excellent wildlife-watching opportunities is the outdoor recreation and demonstration area known as Land Between the Lakes on the border between Kentucky and Tennessee. An outgrowth of one of the most far-reaching development projects in history that dammed the Tennessee and Cumberland rivers, it is a wildlife-filled wooded peninsula that lies between two lakes, Lake Barkley and Kentucky Lake.

Today the forests, fields, and ponds of the peninsula hold sizable populations of the white-tailed and fallow deer, wild turkeys, Canada geese, hawks, eagles, and bobcats that are common in river and lake areas of the southeast. The lake edges are home to raccoons, otters, and beavers.

Many people visit the area by boat to explore its thirty-five hundred miles of undeveloped shoreline. "Most people," said Dennis Sharp, Fish and Wildlife Supervisor of the recreation area, "are surprised to learn that these two lakes with all their indentations have a longer shoreline than Lake Superior." Boaters who steer their craft into these hidden coves may see some of the waterside wildlife. Other visitors go wildlife watching on 140 miles of hiking trails and thirty miles of horse trails.

Raccoon

Look for raccoons along the lakeshore or near a creek. Raccoons are devoted to seafood such as crayfish, frogs, fish, and other freshwater animals, so you will find them close to the water. In fact, it is so natural for a raccoon to hunt near water that a raccoon in captivity will dunk its food into water, probably to mimic the way it would normally pull fish and other prey from a river, lake, or stream.

The northern raccoon, the species that inhabits the United States, is a furry animal with a band of black hairs under the eyes, an appearance that has prompted some people to liken the raccoon to a miniature thief in a mask. Its other trademark is the series of black rings (usually five to seven) that encircle its bushy gray-brown tail.

One of the most remarkable features of the raccoon is its paws. Its forepaws have long flexible fingers with sharp claws at their tips. The claws help it climb rapidly into a tree to escape danger or to return to its den in a tree cavity. Its agile fingers and claws also help the raccoon grab its aquatic prey, clean it, wash it, and eat it.

Raccoons handle objects almost as skillfully as monkeys do. On land the raccoon reaches into crevices in rocks and uses its paws to dig up the ground. Once the raccoon gets hold of something that might be edible, its body stiffens and it lifts the object to sniff it. Its sense of smell is acute. If the food passes the smell test, the raccoon eats it, chewing the item thoroughly instead of gulping it down as do many animals. It carefully separates the shell and hard parts of crustaceans, leaving the indigestible parts behind as so-called coon signs; these may give you a clue that a raccoon is in the neighborhood.

Otter

Whereas the raccoon forages along the water's edge, the river otter spends most of its time in the shallow water near the shore where it hunts for crayfish, crabs, fish, clams, frogs, and snails.

An otter has almost as much dexterity with its forepaws as does the raccoon and can use its toes like fingers in spite of the webbing between the toes. It can pick up a small shellfish in its paws or play with a stone.

A talented swimmer, the otter's sleek body, smooth hair, and powerful muscles send the streamlined animal zipping through the water. Otters can stay underwater from six to eight minutes at a time. When they dive, special adaptations permit them to close their ears and nostrils tightly to keep the water out.

River otters hunt chiefly at night, particularly when the moon is shining brightly. During the daytime you may see them in isolated areas where they are not disturbed, hunting or sunning themselves on a rock. When hunting, the otter waits at the water's edge; when it sees a fish swim by, it slips smoothly into the water, takes short, powerful strokes to overtake its quarry, and catches the fish or other prey with its teeth. The otter's remarkable eyes adapt to the difference in the refractive qualities of air and water and its vision is keen in either medium.

Although an otter sometimes catches a swift fish like a trout, it more often captures slower fish. In shallow water it will drive a school of fish into an inlet by slapping the water with its tail, then chase the fish to a corner where the otter catches up with its quarry. It eats small fish while swimming on its back, holding its catch in its forepaws; a large fish it carries to land. Otters make their homes in well-hidden burrows in bank vegetation or under overhanging tree roots, or in the remodeled home of a beaver or muskrat.

Barred Owl

As at many rivers and lakes, animals of field and forest are not far away from the water. For instance, at Woodlands Nature Center we walked in to find Wally Brines, staff naturalist, holding aloft a gloved hand—a hand that had a barred owl perched on it. The bird cocked its head and stared at the group that gathered around it.

While he kept a firm grip on the owl's tether, the naturalist told his wide-eyed audience of the bird's habits. The barred owl, he said, is one of the most common owls in southern swamps and river bottoms, watery habitats that provide it with its favorite prey: crayfish and frogs. The owl rarely builds its own nest; instead it makes use of a tree hollow vacated by another occupant such as a hawk, crow, or squirrel to safeguard the two or three eggs that the female lays.

Fallow Deer

From the nature center trails lead outward to fields and forests where you may observe wildlife. We caught sight of a fallow deer grazing in a field. The big buck had a magnificent rack of antlers and a gray-brown coat. Spotting our car, it raised its head, took one look, and trotted away toward a line of trees.

How does a fallow deer compare with the more common whitetail? we wondered. "The fallow deer is about the same size as the whitetail," explained Scott Seiber, a community relations specialist at Land Between the Lakes, "but it has keener eyesight. Experiments prove that most deer are unable to distinguish a person standing still from the general background. A fallow deer, however, can pick out the figure of a person from the background even though the person remains motionless." The fallow deer buck also has a larger set of antlers than a whitetail and its tines are flatter, more like a moose's antlers.

Like the white-tailed deer, fallow deer usually live in large herds that consist of females and their offspring. Adult males live in groups of their own but join the female herd for the rutting, or mating, season.

"We have about five hundred of them in the recreation area," Scott added, "one of the largest herds in the country. The two species do not compete with each other very much because the fallow deer is primarily a grazer and the whitetail is a browser. You'll often see fallow deer grazing in groups in a field, while the whitetails stay along field edges and woods."

The fallow deer is not native to this country, Scott said, but originated in the Mediterranean region. It became a favorite of European aristocrats who kept the deer for their private estate herds. It was later introduced in other countries and was brought to this area about 1920.

He went on to explain how the resource managers practice land-use techniques to encourage deer and other wildlife to live in this part of the park. We drove through meadows that were mowed in strips, one strip cut close to the ground, the next growing waist-high.

"Strip mowing provides good habitat for the deer and wild turkey," Scott explained. "The animals feed on the cutover area but can easily escape into the high grass if a predator comes around." Other fields, he said, were planted in winter wheat, corn, or grain sorghum, depending on the season of year, to provide a feeding ground for wildlife and waterfowl.

CHAPTER
5

Prairies and Plains

RIVERS

The web of rivers that fans out across the midsection of the United States provides a drainage system for the country's central low-lands, a region that extends from the Appalachian Mountains in the East to the Rocky Mountains in the West. Major strands of this web are the Mississippi River and its tributaries. If you could look down on the Mississippi River system from above it would look like a glistening two-dimensional tree with wide-spreading branches.

This river system is the end result of millions of years of work by the natural forces of ice and water. The ancient seas that once covered this huge basin of the midcontinent deposited layer upon layer of sediments that gradually hardened into lime-stone, sandstone, and shale. Later the great glaciers pushed their way across the landscape, reaching as far as present-day Ohio, Indiana, and Illinois. As the ice melted, surging meltwaters imprinted the Mississippi, Ohio, Missouri, and other rivers upon the land.

Today you can see numerous signs of this ancient glacial action as you travel the northern states of the region. Much of Minnesota, Wisconsin, and Michigan is underlaid by a jumble of rock and gravel left behind by the glaciers. What seems to be a low ridge actually may be a moraine, residue left by the retreat-ing mass of ice. A sandy beach may be the remains of a glacier that once stood at this spot. A stream winds through a valley that seems too big for it—the sweeping valley was originally con-toured by a huge deluge of meltwater that bulldozed its way through, leaving the wide valley behind.

As we visited national parks, national wildlife refuges, and state parks in the Mississippi River basin we soon understood why the Indians called this mighty river the Father of Waters. From its source at Lake Itasca in northern Minnesota to its fan-shaped delta below New Orleans, the Mississippi flows for 2,350 miles, the longest river in the United States and the second longest in the world (only the Nile in Egypt is longer). The basin of this central water highway blankets all or part of thirty-one states, a region that produces three-fourths of the nation's industrial and agricultural output.

Even the tributaries of the Mississippi River are super-sized. The Missouri River, which rises in the Rocky Mountains near the Canadian border, is only a few miles shorter than the Mississippi itself and drains all or part of ten states. Its erosive action on the land it flows through has given it the name of Big Muddy—said to be "too thick to drink and too thin to plow." When the Missouri joins the Mississippi seventeen miles north of St. Louis, its chocolate-colored stream flows along for miles before it fully mixes with the clearer Mississippi waters.

The Ohio River, which meets the Mississippi farther south at Cairo, Illinois, is only one-third as long as the Mississippi or Missouri but contributes twice the volume of water. We climbed to the top of a concrete observation platform at Point Defiance State Park to see where the two rivers join. The Mississippi, discolored from the silt of the Missouri, flowed along the west bank while the clearer water of the Ohio flowed in from the east, the two bands eventually mixing downstream.

On occasion the Mississippi River system floods and overflows its banks with disastrous results. The floods usually come when deep winter snows melt and spring rains swell the tributaries, magnifying the volume of water in the main stream and leading to flooding on the lower Mississippi. Wildlife as well as humans become victims in a massive flood. As the waters rise, animals such as deer that live at ground level take flight, moving toward higher ground. Animals accustomed to spending part of their days in trees—raccoons, squirrels, opossums—take to the branches to wait out the floodwaters. Even after the flood the wildlife may remain hungry because their food sources have been swept away. The worst hit are rodents like the groundhog, badger, and field mouse that, unable to outrun the floodwaters, drown in their burrows.

In the last fifty years man has tried mightily to moderate these floods using dams, levees, dredging, and floodways. By these methods engineers are learning to control the future rampages of "Old Man River."

The slow-flowing Mississippi River not only serves as an important transportation corridor, it also plays an important role as one of four major bird migration routes that span the United States from north to south.

Every spring and fall the river and its valley provide resting and feeding grounds for millions of migrating birds, many of them flying from their summer habitat in Canada to winter quarters on the East Coast or in the southern United States, in the Caribbean, Mexico, or Central and South America.

A number of natural preserves—national wildlife refuges, national parks, national forests, and state and local parks—provide stopover points for this impressive migration. We visited the largest of these, the Upper Mississippi River National Wildlife and Fish Refuge. The longest refuge in the country, it stretches in several segments for 284 miles along the Mississippi River through four states: Minnesota, Wisconsin, Iowa, and Illinois. Its three and a half million annual visitors make it the most heavily visited refuge in the country.

"On this part of the river the Mississippi is no longer free-flowing but is more like a series of stairsteps created by dams that back up pools of water from ten to thirty miles long," explained Refuge Manager Jim Lennartson. Eleven dams, he said, were constructed in the 1930s on this stretch of the river by the U. S. Army Corps of Engineers to back up lakes deep enough to allow towboats to push their barges up these watery stairsteps through a system of locks to Minneapolis.

The backed-up lakes brought another result as well. As the water rose behind each dam it spread into the river valley to form islands, marshes, backwater lakes, inlets, shallows, sandbars, and sloughs (pronounced "slews") that provide aquatic habitats for a wide variety of wildlife. Before the dams were built, water levels fluctuated so widely that vegetation would grow one year but be drowned out the next. Now the dam operators can control the river levels better, Jim said, and habitats survive from one season to another. As a result, the refuge provides a stopover point for more than 270 species of birds, as well as a home for

canvasback duck and drake

fifty kinds of mammals, forty-five different reptiles and amphibians, and more than 113 species of fish.

Canvasback

"About three-fourths of all the continental canvasback ducks use this refuge as a resting and feeding area during their fall migration to the Atlantic and Gulf coasts," Jim told us. The canvasback, the swiftest flyer of all the ducks, migrates from the lakes and marshy ponds of the United States and Canadian prairies to winter in the bays and inlets of the mid-Atlantic and Gulf coasts. The Mississippi Valley is an important segment of this migration route.

The canvasback, whose body is mostly white with a reddish brown head, is a diving duck that feeds on aquatic plants such as

tundra swan

wild celery that grow in the shallow lakes and inlets. The canvas-back can dive as deep as thirty feet in search of such underwater salad.

Legs of diving ducks like the canvasback are placed farther back on its body than the legs of surface-feeding ducks. In this way it can better thrust itself into a dive and propel itself to the bottom. As a result of this leg positioning, however, the diving duck has an awkward waddling gait when on land.

Diving ducks need a long run to become airborne, their feet pattering along the top of the water surface until the beat of their wings becomes strong enough to lift them aloft. A surface-feeding duck, or dabbling duck, on the other hand, explodes from the surface when it takes flight.

Chilly weather does not bother a duck like the canvasback. Its waterproof feathers trap the air in and keep the water out. A layer of fat and specially adapted blood circulation through its feet are additional ways the duck minimizes heat loss.

Tundra Swan

Another notable migrating bird that relies on the Upper Mississippi sanctuary is the tundra or whistling swan. This elegant white bird is one of the migration champions of the bird world, flying from its summer home on the coastline of Alaska and northern Canada to its winter home around the Chesapeake Bay—a journey of more than five thousand miles.

In spring and fall you may spot flocks of these large white birds flying in V-shaped formations similar to that of the Canada goose. The tundra swan is larger than the Canada goose and is all white except for its black bill and a small yellow spot near each of its eyes. A mellow high-pitched call of *hoo-hoo-hoo*, rather than a harsh honk, will be the tip-off that the flock you see high in the sky is a group of tundra swans and not Canada geese.

In formation the swans are usually led by an experienced member of the flock, their wings beating slowly and regularly, their necks outstretched toward their destination. Young swans, or cygnets, are placed in the less turbulent air between the older birds, thus giving the young ones an easier time of it.

As many as twelve thousand tundra swans have been observed at one feeding area along the Upper Mississippi. The swan eats worms, shellfish, and the tubers of water plants such as arrowhead, dipping its beak and neck deep into the water to reach to the bottom.

Other Bird Life

Jim pointed out that these Mississippi backwaters have become even more important in recent years to migrating birds as nearby states have drained their wetlands for farming and for industrial development. The Upper Mississippi is becoming an oasis in America's heartland because many other streams have been channelized, bottomland forests have vanished, and natural lakes and potholes have been filled.

"The best way to see this long refuge is by boat," advised Hank Schneider, an outdoor recreation planner. "That way you can get back in the quiet sloughs and have your best chance to see birds, other animals, and aquatic plants." If you don't have a boat, Hank said, the next best way to see the refuge is by car following the Great River Road as we were doing, stopping at overlooks along the way. This designated scenic road follows the entire length of the Mississippi River from its source to its delta in Louisiana. On the section we followed, the road occasionally ran high atop steep bluffs and gave us a sweeping view of the river and the refuge.

Bird life was abundant. Squadrons of herring gulls wheeled above the dam pools. We watched for a while as the gulls searched the river for fish, then flew inland to check out nearby plowed fields for grubs and worms. At night they return to a roosting place where they group together. Herring gulls mate for life and return to the same nesting site year after year.

Surface-feeding ducks such as wigeons, gadwalls, and teal stuck their heads in the water and upended in search of a tasty bit of plant food.

Deep in the marshland along the river, normally out of sight, are the tan-colored bittern and the secretive rail. The bittern is well camouflaged in its environment; if alarmed, this bird freezes in position, pointing its head and bill upward so that its entire body blends in with the tall reeds around it.

Great blue herons stood on gangly legs, while great egrets, their white feathers contrasting with the green vegetation, took wing. Hundreds of herons and egrets, Hank told us, raise their young in several large rookeries in remote areas of the refuge.

We were disappointed not to see the colorful wood duck, a waterfowl that feeds in small pools or timbered areas. Considered the most gaudily colored of all the ducks, it glows with iridescent hues. The wood duck feeds on insects and duckweed when it is in the water and on acorns, beechnuts, hickory nuts, and wild grapes when it forages in the forest.

As you drive the Great River Road north and south from the Upper Mississippi refuge, you will find bird-watching opportunities at other national wildlife refuges and national and state parks along the Mississippi flyway. The Mark Twain National Wildlife Refuge, for example, offers good habitat for migrating ducks and some three hundred bald eagles that winter there. Reelfoot Lake

National Wildlife Refuge at the Kentucky-Tennessee border, an oxbow lake that was once a bend in the Mississippi River, draws outdoor enthusiasts to view record numbers of ducks as well as migrating raptors.

Minnesota Valley National Wildlife Refuge near Minneapolis is not only a popular spot for the birds of the flyway, it also preserves a calcareous fen, a rare type of wetland plant community. Whereas a bog is acidic, a fen is alkaline. Water bubbling to the surface from the limestone beneath is rich in calcium and magnesium bicarbonate. Calcium-tolerant plants that grow in a fen, like Minnesota Valley's white lady's slipper and sticky false asphodel, are found in only a few places and are therefore listed as species of special concern.

Shoreline Plants

Hank pointed out that the aquatic vegetation that grows along its shoreline makes the Upper Mississippi a productive feeding ground for waterfowl and fish. Water plants, he explained, are as valuable to a lake or a river as is grass to a meadow or trees to a forest.

Closest to the bank is weedy growth that provides food and shelter for fish as well as host plants for insect larvae. Bass and sunfish usually locate their nests in weeds along the shore. Northern pike spawn in these marshy areas in early spring.

As the submerged plants grow they absorb phosphates, nitrates, and other nutrient elements from the water and soil. If such water plants should be destroyed, a heavy growth or "bloom" of algae may follow as the algae takes advantage of the surplus nutrients usually taken up by the plants. Water plants also add oxygen to the water, thus making it livable for fish and other aquatic life.

The shallows a little farther out from shore are the domain of plants called *emergents*. These plants, such as the cattail, have their roots firmly anchored in submerged soil while parts of their stems, leaves, and flowers are held above the surface.

Sedges grow here too. Sedges are high, grasslike plants that have narrow leaves arranged in threes. Sedges have a stem that is triangular shaped; rushes like the bulrush, on the other hand, have a rounded stem like a knitting needle. One easy way to remember the difference is that "sedges have edges and rushes are round." Bulrushes produce seeds and tubers eaten by ducks and provide excellent shelter for broods of ducklings.

Arrowhead displays its arrow-shaped leaves in the shallows as does the lotus, which lifts its large round leaves and yellow flowers two to three feet above the water.

Beyond the emergents but still in relatively shallow water are floating plants such as the water lily. The lily, moored to its thick root stalk, is custom-made for floating. It spreads its broad leaves on top of the water where they can soak up the maximum sunshine. Their waxy coating prevents them from becoming waterlogged either from the water below or from rain that pelts down on them. Lily pads often play host to other life as well. Newly hatched tadpoles hang with specialized suckers from the underside of a lily pad for protection.

Fish Life

Water's-edge vegetation provides good habitat for fish. "The largest number of visitors here at the refuge are fishermen," Hank said, noting that some ten million Midwesterners live within one hundred miles of the Mississippi River. Knowledgeable fishermen cast their lines in the turbulent waters just below the dams, in backwater sloughs, or channels between the river islands; these are favorite spots for fish.

Among the most popular sport fish are the walleyed pike, sauger, and largemouth bass. The walleye and the sauger, both in the perch family, resemble each other although the sauger is smaller. Both have a splotchy appearance, a sleek shape, and sharp teeth with which they prey on other fish. The walleye averages three pounds in weight and can grow to about forty inches in length; the sauger is only one-third that size. Both are prized by anglers as a fighting quarry. The largemouth bass is a predator fish as well but has a more varied diet that includes insects, frogs, crayfish, and snakes as well as other fish. Olive to black on its back, it has an irregular dark stripe from gill to tail and averages two pounds in weight.

Crappies, perch, and sunfish also abound, as do several bottom fish including the carp and catfish. The carp is a sluggish fish that roots up plants from the bottom, muddying the water and occasionally smothering with silt the spawn left by other fish. Carp winter deep in holes, emerging to forage on plants, worms, and crustaceans. In the spring a twenty-pound female carp deposits as many as two million eggs.

The catfish, too, can get along in murky water and is not finicky about its diet. This lack of discrimination has long kept the catfish in low repute. This view is changing, however. Surprisingly, Americans eat enough of the freshwater catfish to earn it sixth place in economic value among food fishes, after salmon, tuna, flounder, haddock, and halibut, which are all saltwater fish.

Mussels

Many other aquatic animals besides fish inhabit the river currents. We saw one interesting example when we canoed the upper St. Croix River with Ranger Dennis Kaleta. The St. Croix is a scenic river that forms much of the border between Wisconsin and Minnesota. As we paddled across a shoal area in the stream we looked into the clear water to see a multitude of shells lying on the bottom, some of them light colored, others darkish.

"Those are mussels," Dennis said. "To grow they attach themselves to the rocks on the river bottom or to other mussels. Forty of the forty-eight species of freshwater mussels known in this country are found in the St. Croix."

The mussel, he explained, looks much like a clam and is even mistakenly called a clam by many local people. It is a bivalve mollusk, a water animal that has a soft body within a hard shell. It embeds itself in the river bottom with its shell partly open, the hinged end pointing upward. A filter feeder, the mussel lives on a diet of microorganisms it gleans from the currents that flow past it. One siphon takes in food and water while an output siphon releases wastes downstream.

The mussels of the St. Croix, we discovered, have fanciful names such as "heelsplitter," "monkey face," "pimpleback," "elephant ear," "hickory nut," and "elk toe"—these names giving a clue to their appearance. "All are protected," Dennis commented, "although some are abundant and some are rare." One kind, he said, the Higgins Eye, is so rare that it has been designated as an

mussels

endangered species. "We have one of the few healthy populations in the world on the St. Croix so we want to be particularly
protective of that one."

A remarkable characteristic of mussels is that each kind
depends for reproduction on a fish or other aquatic host. Its life
cycle begins when a female mussel draws in the sperm released
into the water by a nearby male mussel, thus fertilizing its eggs.
The eggs develop for several weeks, growing into larvae called
glochidia, tiny mollusks that have minute hooks along the edge of
their developing shell.

When the time is right, the mother mussel contracts both its
input and output valves and expels the young glochidia into the
water through its output siphon. The glochidia of one species,
the Higgins Eye, if not eaten by waiting fish or crustaceans, survive by attaching themselves to a sauger or drumfish. These two
fish (evidently only these two) serve as hosts for the next stage

of a mussel's growth. The glochidia embed themselves in the gills of the fish, where they may draw sustenance from the fish and are carried by it to another location. Without the sauger and the drumfish the mussel population could not survive—an example of the interdependence of one species on another.

After about a month the young mussels drop from the fish's gills and settle on the riverbed where they must find rocks or other shells to cling to. It takes another one to eight years for the young to reach maturity and repeat this extraordinary life cycle.

Riverside Vegetation

We learned what a rich variety of vegetation grows along a river on the damp day we took a nature walk with a group of park visitors along the St. Croix. Our guide was Tom Diener, a personable naturalist who serves at St. Croix State Park in Minnesota.

Tom pointed out a slender tree whose bark was dark gray but looked almost black in the dim light of the forest. The bark had shallow interlocking cracks in it. "Black ash," Tom told our group. "The Indians learned how to peel off layers of black ash in narrow strips and weave it into baskets. My wife has learned the art and her black ash baskets last a long time."

We walked past a basswood tree, a large specimen that had a heart-shaped leaf with serrated edges. Its seeds, which grow in clusters of three or four, twirl as they fall to the ground like a helicopter rotor. Its flowers attract bees, which use the nectar to make excellent honey. The flowers also perfume the air on warm summer nights. The Indians had a use for this tree, too, Tom added: They cut away a layer of bark and soaked it in water to peel away the inner bark, which they used to make a strong twine.

"And here's one the deer like—the hazel," he said, pointing to a six-foot-high bush. "I'll show you why." He picked off one of the light green burrs that hung in clusters below large oval leaves. Using his knife, he peeled off the sticky covering to expose a dark brown nut. He crushed it between two flat rocks and handed out pieces of the sweet-tasting nut all around. Although most of us were familiar with hazelnuts, also called filberts, it was a good chance to see them growing in the wild.

Picking a red berry from another tree, Tom handed it to a young girl in our group, asking her to taste it. She did—and wrinkled her nose in disgust. "You're right, it doesn't taste so good, does it?" he laughed. The Indians didn't make use of it for its taste but for another reason. Some say the juice of the mountain ash berry could numb an area or reduce the pain from an injury or a toothache."

Down close to the ground Tom pointed out the Virginia creeper, a ground-hugging five-leafed vine, and the bloodroot. The bloodroot, he said, is well named because its root oozes a red sap that appears like blood.

"Here's another plant that's well named," he continued, "the sensitive fern. You see how green it is now during the summertime. But when the first frost comes, this fern turns brown overnight. The early explorers and trappers who knew these forests used the sensitive fern as a weather indicator."

Bald Eagle

"There are about twenty nesting pairs of bald eagles along the riverway." Pegg Peterson, a National Park Service ranger on the St. Croix, was telling us about the river on a boat trip through The Dalles, a beautiful high-walled canyon downstream from where we saw the mussels. Bald eagles, Pegg reminded us, have few natural enemies. But they do need a special kind of environment—quiet isolation and tall, mature trees in which to build their huge nests.

Over the years, she related, the wilderness in our country was cleared to make way for towns and farms. Virgin forests were cut for lumber and for fuel. In the process the isolation of the wild was shattered and lofty nesting trees grew scarce. With their normal lifestyle thus disrupted, bald eagles declined in number. Meanwhile, these proud birds of prey became prey themselves. Many were shot by farmers, ranchers, and hunters. Egg collectors robbed their nests.

Even greater damage occurred after World War II with the introduction of the pesticide DDT. Broadly effective and believed to be relatively nontoxic, it was applied extensively on croplands throughout the country where it was credited with saving millions of dollars in produce. Only later did other environmental consequences come to light. DDT residues could wash into lakes and streams and be absorbed by the aquatic plants and organisms that sustain the fish. The fish, in turn, were eaten by the eagles. The birds subsequently laid eggs whose shells were so thin they were often crushed during incubation. The eagle reproduction rate dropped. By the early 1970s biologists estimated that fewer than three thousand bald eagles were left in the lower forty-eight states.

Today, Pegg said, increased protection for the birds, a decline in the use of DDT as a pesticide, and an increased awareness of the habitat eagles need have brought about a threefold increase in the number of bald eagles nesting along the St. Croix.

With its majestic proportions, the bald eagle is one of nature's most imposing birds of prey. A male measures almost three feet from head to tail, weighs eight to ten pounds, and spreads its wings about six and one-half feet. Females grow even larger, up to three and one-half feet long. The bird's dark brown body and huge, pale eyes, fierce yellow beak, and grasping talons add to its formidable appearance. Its distinctive white head and tail feathers appear only after the bird is four or five years old, replacing a mottled brown coloring.

The bald eagle eats many small mammals, reptiles, and birds. It especially likes fish, and will rob an osprey of a fish it has caught. Eagles often build their nests, or *eyries*, near a river where fish are plentiful.

With the bald eagle making a comeback, visitors to the St. Croix and other rivers and lakes where the bird has found a home may be treated to the sight of an eagle swooping down from its high perch to snatch a fish from the water, then arc back to its nest. Those who appreciate the wildlife along a river can once again thrill to the performance of this unique bird that is found only on the North American continent.

LAKES

No one can accuse whoever named the Great Lakes of making an overstatement: these five huge lakes together hold one-fifth of all the surface fresh water on earth and fully 95 percent of all the surface fresh water in the United States.

The lakes cover ninety-five thousand square miles, an area greater than the combined areas of Illinois and Michigan. If you emptied these inland seas and poured all the water over the forty-eight contiguous states, it would inundate them to a depth of ten feet.

The five lakes—Superior, Michigan, Huron, Erie, and Ontario—extend eight hundred miles from west to east and provide about eight thousand miles of shoreline for Americans and Canadians to use and enjoy. Some 13 percent of Americans live around the Great Lakes, demographers say, while fully one-third of all Canadians live relatively close to the lakes.

You can think of the five lakes as five bathtubs filled with water, each standing next to the other, each successive one a little lower than one before it. This chain of lakes has provided a water highway into the interior of the continent since the days when French fur trappers, the *voyageurs*, braved the lakes in their fragile bark canoes. From Lake Superior in the west to Lake Ontario in the east, and thence through the St. Lawrence Seaway to the Atlantic Ocean, the Great Lakes form the world's largest freshwater transportation network.

Glacial Geology

The Great Lakes owe their shape and size to the bulldozing action of the great glaciers that once pushed their way across this region. When the mighty masses of ice retreated, meltwater gradually filled the hollows that the glaciers had scraped out and the Great Lakes were born. Thousands of smaller lakes that speckle Michigan, Wisconsin, Minnesota, and North Dakota were formed in the same way. We could understand why Minnesota is known as "the land of ten thousand lakes."

In Wisconsin, at Kettle Moraine State Forest, we came upon some of the "footprints" that glaciers make and learned a new vocabulary of glacial terms. Here you discover glacial lakes and ponds that have remained virtually undisturbed since they took shape ten thousand years ago.

In few places are more reminders of the Ice Age preserved for the public in one relatively small area than at this Wisconsin park, located near Campbellsport, fifty miles northeast of Milwaukee. So significant are the topographic features at Kettle Moraine that the forest has been designated as one of nine sites that together comprise the Ice Age Scientific Reserve, a unit of the National Park System. The nine sites are spread across south-

A reminder of the glacial age, this pothole in a rock at Wisconsin's Interstate State Park was once submerged below raging meltwaters. The small stone or grindstone the visitor holds in her hand was spun within the pothole by the force of the water, boring like a drill into the rock.

ern and central Wisconsin and preserve outstanding glacial features. Eventually, a trail about one thousand miles long will link these Ice Age units.

"You'll see examples of most of the major topographic features left by the glaciers," said Roger Reif, the enthusiastic park naturalist, as he plotted out an auto tour that would take us on a forty-mile circle tour of the surrounding landscape. To help us identify the glacial features we would see on our tour, Roger described each one and told us how it was created. These features had been formed, he said, as the huge wall of ice advanced and retreated across the land.

During an advance the glacial ice moved slowly forward— shearing off and flattening hills and bluffs, scratching, scraping, crushing, gouging, and grinding up bedrock into large and small pieces. When temperatures warmed and the glacial front retreated, this ground-up debris was left behind in heaps, ridges, or mounds atop the gently rolling land. This layer of rocks and gravel, a layer that varies in thickness from a few inches to a hundred yards or more, is the legacy of the glaciers.

Before starting on our tour, we walked out to the broad observation deck of the visitor center. Diagrams identify the glacial features that you see from the deck. The visitor center itself, Roger told us, was built atop a *terminal moraine*, a ridge of debris that marked a glacier's farthest advance.

With our map and tour folder in hand and our eye on the green signs that marked the route, we departed. We made our first stop for a close-up look at a *kame* (pronounced came) we had seen from the visitor center. Our folder explained that the gumdrop-shaped hill was formed when rocks and gravel fell down a vertical shaft in the thick ice sheet and were left behind when the glacier melted back.

Our next stop was a *kettle lake* named Butler Lake. A kettle lake is a body of water that fills the depression left long ago when a huge chunk of ice was left behind by a retreating glacier. Covered with debris that slowed its melt rate, the chunk sank slowly into the surrounding silt to form the shores of the lake, its waters filling the depression. It is now an oval, tree-ringed body of water—today it was occupied by two fishermen in a boat trying their luck in its ancient depths.

But the kettle lake is not the only feature you see here. Stretching back from one side of the lake is an *esker*, a narrow, gravelly ridge. An esker is, in effect, an upside-down streambed. As the glacier melted, the meltwater ran beneath the ice sheet in torrents. This debris-laden water carried with it a tumbling mass of rocks that ground itself into gravel that piled up in its streambed. When the glacier receded, the ridge of gravel remained. We walked the trail that now leads along the rounded crest of Parnell Esker that stands some twenty feet above the surrounding terrain, the residue of an ice sheet of ages past.

Down the road we passed a scene better known in Wisconsin than its glacial remains—a grazing dairy herd. In the pasture, with the grass neatly clipped around it by the grazing cows, stood a pink-colored boulder the size of a compact car. This was an *erratic*, a chunk of granite that had been transported by a glacier from its place of origin many miles to the north in Canada.

Another geologic feature created by glacial action is a *pothole*. The deepest known pothole in the country is the "Bottomless Pit" at Minnesota Interstate State Park, sixty feet deep and twelve to fifteen feet wide. This and other potholes were created by an eddy from a glacial torrent whirling in one spot. Sand and silt in the water acted like a drill, biting into the basalt. If a rock, called a grindstone, fell into the hole, it too was spun around, enlarging the pothole and smoothing the sides of the grindstone. As the river flow slowed or lessened, the wearing process stopped and the pothole was left high and dry. We saw many such potholes, some with grindstones the size of cannonballs still lying at the bottom.

Duckweed

One of the deepest kettles in the Kettle Moraine preserve greeted us at our next stop. More symmetrical than the first kettle, the Greenbush Kettle is almost as deep as it is wide. From its steep sides you can deduce that a large chunk of ice resisted melting for a long time as its weight pressed it deeply into the surrounding silt like an ice cube melting in warm mud.

The day we saw the lake it was covered with duckweed. The light green duckweed has the distinction of being among the smallest and simplest flowering plants in the world. Each small plant in this waterborne carpet has a buoyant, disclike leaf that has a threadlike root hanging from it into the water. Its leaves contain air-filled sacs that keep them afloat. Tiny flowers bloom along the thin edge of the plant that gets its name because it is a favorite food source for some ducks.

As a finale to our auto tour of glacial phenomena, we climbed a sixty-foot wooden tower built atop a moraine that reached the highest elevation in the state forest (1,113 feet above sea level). In one direction we gazed at other tree-covered moraines that mark the farthest forward movement of the great glacier. In another direction lay the vast, now-dry basin that was once Lake Chicago, a predecessor of the present-day Lake Michigan. In yet another direction were the knobs of several of the conical kames we had seen earlier, rounded hills hunching their shoulders above the landscape.

Now, mustering all of our imagination, we directed our gaze upward, to an imaginary point in the sky sixty times higher than the tower on which we were standing. In our minds we filled in the vast area beneath this point with the looming mass of a glacier that once stood there. Only in this way could we capture the power and pressure of the immense sheet of ice that many years ago wrought such changes in the Wisconsin geography.

Plant Succession on Sand Dunes

From the trailhead where we stood the mountain of gleaming sand loomed in front of us. As we started the upward climb the soft sand gave way beneath our feet and trickled over our shoe tops.

"Won't our footsteps leave prints in the sand?" Marge asked Ranger Darryl Blink who was leading us up Mount Baldy as he had led us through Pinhook Bog.

"Not for long," he replied. "This is a wandering dune, continually being pushed forward by the wind. In an hour or so your footprints will be erased."

After a fifteen-minute trudge up the slippery slope we stood at the top of 123-foot Mount Baldy, the largest moving dune at Indiana Dunes National Lakeshore, a park located at the southeastern tip of Lake Michigan. A similar area of windblown sand dunes, Sleeping Bear Dunes National Lakeshore, is farther north on the shore of Lake Michigan.

Only at a few places in the country will you find inland dunes like these along a lake, for they were created by a special set of circumstances. They are souvenirs of the glacial age, their sands the result of rocks ground exceedingly fine, left behind by the ancient ice sheets then subjected to the action of water and wind.

Currents in Lake Michigan start the process of dune building, Darryl explained, as they carry sand southward and deposit it along the shores at the southern end of the lake. Some of the sand is built into sandbars beneath the surface, some is cast up on the beach by the surf. The prevailing winds then whip into

Sand dunes mean playtime at Indiana Dunes National Lakeshore. Prevailing winds that blow across Lake Michigan lift grains of sand from sandbars and beaches and whisk them inland, where they heap up in huge mounds.

action. When wind speeds exceed seven miles per hour, the breeze picks up grains of sand and rolls or bounces them inland where they pile up against the first obstacle in their way.

The wind continues to shape the dunes. A strong enough wind, Darryl said, can even carve a channel through a low place in a dune ridge, widening and deepening it until it creates a huge rounded bowl called a blowout. If it deepens still more, the sand may be scoured down to the water table to produce an interdunal pond.

As we walked across Mount Baldy's sprawling surface Marge tripped on a snag of wood sticking out of the sand. "Believe it or not," Darryl said, "that's the top of a dead tree. A dune like this often builds up around a small forest, covering the trees and killing them. Later, as the wind gradually pushes the dune inland,

Marram grass is often the first plant to take root in a sand dune, beginning the stabilization process that will eventually halt the dune's movement. Rhizomes and roots of a single marram grass plant may spread as much as twenty feet in all directions.

the dead trees below are uncovered once more and the dead branches protrude through the surface."

We walked to the farthest edge of the dune to look down a 45-degree slope of sand—the leading edge of the dune. It looked like a scene from the Sahara until we looked down. Far below we saw the tops of other trees, spread out like a carpet, awaiting their turn to be smothered by the advancing dune. Darryl pointed out a tree part way down the steep slope. It was already two-thirds covered with sand. "I have a photograph from a few years ago that shows that tree standing untouched," he said. "We calculate that Mount Baldy moves about four to five feet each year."

Other dunes, however, become stabilized by nature into *fore-dunes* through a process of plant succession. To learn the succes-

In the process of beach succession, dunes are gradually transformed from sandy hills to hardwood forests. Shown here are some of the plants that have a role in beach succession: marram grass, bluestem bunchgrass, cottonwood, juniper, and ironwood.

sion story we walked the West Beach Succession Trail that leads inland from West Beach, a popular swimming and sunbathing location at the lakeshore. The self-guiding trail begins at a beach and ends in a shady oak forest, tracing a process that takes years to evolve. Succession is the means by which a group of plants or animals in a particular place is gradually replaced over time by other, sometimes very different, natural communities.

Although succession is now taught routinely in biology classes, it was a controversial new idea at the turn of the century when a University of Chicago professor, Henry Chandler Cowles, first brought his students to this shore of Lake Michigan. Using the area as an outdoor laboratory to demonstrate how plant succession worked, he achieved worldwide recognition not only for himself but also for this sand dune country. Because of Cowles's work the dunes became known as the birthplace of the science called *ecology*.

We started with several plants at the beach that are the first to slow the shifting sands. Seaside spurge is an annual plant that grows close to the ground. Sea rocket is a succulent whose leaves hold water and whose roots reach deep down to the water table below. Wormwood, a shorter cousin of the desert sagebrush, gets its foothold just behind the beach.

Another plant, marram grass, not only survives the barrage of sand whipped up by the wind, it actually thrives on being buried. As you walk the trail a few green sprigs are all you see. But the business end of this plant is below the surface where specialized underground stems called *rhizomes* spread. At least a dozen *internodes*, the sections between each stem joint, develop each year. If the sand piles up quickly, the internodes will be lengthy; if summer breezes are gentle and the sand piles up slowly, the plant's growth slows and the internodes will be short. The rhizomes and internodes of a single marram grass plant may spread up to twenty feet in different directions. A typical foredune is held together beneath the surface by a dense network of these underground threads.

One or two other grasses such as sand reed grass and little bluestem bunchgrass join the marram grass, paving the way for shrubs and vines whose roots absorb nutrients left by the decomposing grasses, the first step toward building soil.

Next in the line of succession is the cottonwood tree. We recognized the heart-shaped leaf of this tree that also grows along dry washes in the desert Southwest. The cottonwood, once it gains a foothold, exhibits an unusual characteristic. As the tree's branches are buried by moving sand, they begin to function instead as roots. New branches sprout above ground and the tree continues to grow. What looked to us like cottonwoods that were only a foot or two high were actually the exposed tips of giant living cottonwoods that towered some sixty feet tall but were submerged in the sand.

As the grasses, shrubs, and cottonwoods go through their life cycle of death and decay they contribute to a richer soil and cooler, moister, and less windblown conditions at ground level. In this improved environment the arctic bearberry grows, providing a good seedbed for jack pine, white pine, common juniper, and red cedar, which in turn prepare the way for other common dune trees such as black oak, white oak, and basswood. Trees and shrubs like sassafras, dogwood, witch hazel, ironwood, and serviceberry form an understory, providing all the attributes of a true forest.

Plant Succession on an Island

At Stockton Island, within Apostle Islands National Lakeshore in western Lake Superior, we saw another example of habitat evolution as Seasonal Ranger Terry Dunn led us on a two-mile nature walk. On our hike we circled a knob of land that juts out from the main island, a knob called Presque Isle.

"It's well named," Terry said. "It means 'nearly an island' in French. Actually, this knob of land is a *tombolo*. A tombolo forms when sand is washed in by lake currents and forms a sand bridge that links what used to be a small isle to the main island. The beaches, sandspits, and tombolos you see on the island are literally rivers of sand, moved along by currents of wind and water."

The tombolo has undergone a process of plant succession that has occurred over more than five thousand years, she explained. The open sand of the tombolo was first colonized by a community of beach grass, beach heather, dwarf juniper, blueberries, and roses. As that community matured it created conditions conducive to a succession of plants such as pines and birches. This process continued until some dunes were able to support a "climax forest" of red and white pines. It continues today as plant communities grow and change on the dunes.

Ferns

Moving inland, Terry pointed out a carpet of ferns, fungi, mushrooms, and mosses that grow in the cool, damp interior of the forest. The wildflowers that grow here, she said, bloom in the spring before the trees put out leaves that block the sunlight.

Ferns, she told us, are flowerless plants. Recognizing the different species is a skill that few people have mastered because each fern has its distinctive characteristics. Habitat, of course, has a great influence. Ferns like these grow in the woods; others grow among rocks, in bogs and swamps, along moist stream banks, even on tree trunks. Ferns have many different sizes and shapes. Some are so small they look like moss; others grow so tall they look like trees.

They take different growth forms: lax, erect, clustered, or scattered. The leaf of a fern is called a *frond*; each little leaflet of the frond is a *pinna*. Before we could move farther along the trail, our guide insisted that we learn to recognize the distinctive patterns of three fern species common to the island: the lacy wood fern, the interrupted fern, and the long beech fern. The wood fern has lacy sets of pinnae and grows from two to five feet high. The interrupted fern has fronds that are wide in the middle then taper at the tip and base, while the long beech fern is widest at the base of the frond then tapers toward the top to from a narrow pyramid. Terry pointed out the tiny spore cases on the underside of the leaves of the wood fern. These clusters of sporangia contain tiny fern seeds, called spores, that disperse easily in the wind, a characteristic that helps make ferns one of the most widely distributed plants in the world.

Almost hidden beneath the ferns we noticed what looked like three- to four-inch-high miniature Christmas trees. These, she said, were club moss. Club moss grows so slowly that the three-inch plant we saw had probably been growing for twenty years. The club moss, we decided, was a good example of why park regulations prohibit picking or destroying any of the plants on the island.

Sandhill Crane

On the opposite side of Presque Isle, sandstone ledges and a jumble of rocks formed the shoreline, broadening at one place into a beach. When we walked out on the beach, the sand made a sort of squeaking sound beneath our feet. "Singing sand," Terry explained. "It occurs because the sand is made up of quartz whose grains are round and all about the same size." The round grains, subjected to outside pressure, squeak like a multitude of tiny marbles being forced together.

"We saw two sandhill cranes the other day just up the beach from here," she said. "Come on, let's see if they're still there."

Leaving the trail, we hiked over sandy hillocks for a quarter of a mile. All at once Marge spotted the pair of birds, wading stiff-legged in a bog, jabbing downward with their beaks to capture an insect or grub. "Most sandhills are in Canada at this time of the year," Terry said. "These two are at about the southernmost part of their range."

A smaller cousin of the rare whooping crane, the sandhill crane is three to four feet long and has gray feathers in contrast to the white coloration of the whooper. It does carry the same distinctive red patch atop its head.

Awkward-looking on land with its long, jointed legs, the sandhill is an accomplished flier. On a long migratory flight it flies with a slow, rhythmic flapping of its large wings, moving at about forty-five miles per hour over the landscape and averaging some two hundred miles each day.

When not feeding on small plants, insects, frogs, worms, reptiles, small fish, and eggs, a sandhill may rest or doze a while. Standing on one leg with its head drawn back between its shoulders, it gathers its energy for the next feeding foray. During migration thousands of cranes fly together, the trumpeting sounds of the flock echoing for miles.

Cormorant

Water birds abounded at Rainy Lake, one of four large interlocking lakes that form the heart of Voyageurs National Park, a watery wonderland that lies along the United States-Canadian border of Minnesota. The waters of Voyageurs are part of a tapestry of lakes and rivers, ponds and rapids, that intertwine with those of two nearby wilderness areas: Boundary Waters Canoe Area and Canada's Quetico Provincial Park.

Several ducks paddled near our tour boat, seemingly unconcerned by our approach. If we came too close, though, they upended and disappeared. "Mergansers and goldeneyes," said Bill Gardiner, a veteran ranger and the park's chief naturalist. "Both are diving ducks. Goldeneyes feed on bottom vegetation, while the mergansers feed on fish."

An osprey left its perch on a branch, flew in a wide circle above us to reconnoiter, then dove to the lake surface, splashing into the water in an unsuccessful attempt to grab a fish.

As our tour boat followed the shoreline we looked up to see four cormorants flying by in formation, their slender black bodies silhouetted against the sky. When they fly in groups, cormorants form the same kind of oblique line or ragged V as do geese.

But this sleek hunter has few other similarities to the goose. The cylindrical bill that is hooked at its tip, the bright orange pouch under its chin, and a dark, glossy plumage distinguish the cormorant. You can recognize the bird by the way it perches on a rock, tree stump, or buoy, its body upright and its neck relaxing in the shape of an S. When it takes off from its perch, the cormorant usually dips almost to the surface of the water before lifting into the air; hence the belief that a cormorant "must wet its tail before it can fly."

When hunting, the cormorant skims the surface, scanning the water for a fish. When it spots one, it makes a quick, shallow dive to grab it. With a snap of its bill it stores its prize in the orange pouch. Unlike the pelican that hunts in much the same way, the cormorant can dive beneath the surface and swim a long distance in pursuit of its prey.

Cormorants build a large nest of sticks and grass, the male and female working together. Look for a cormorant's nest on a tree snag on a rocky island that overlooks a good fishing ground. Some nests can be two feet high and two feet in diameter. Both parents help incubate the three or four eggs the female produces each year.

Loon

"Has everyone seen a loon by now?" Bill asked. "There's one to starboard." He indicated a large, gaudily decorated black-and-white bird that was paddling in the water. A rare sight in many parts of the country, loons are common in these north woods. "It's Minnesota's state bird," he said. "You'll see a lot of them in the park."

Loons almost always return to the same lake to nest, usually one pair to a lake. Each pair, Bill continued, usually seeks out its

loon

old nesting site: a mound of turf at the water's edge, a heap of debris, or perhaps a muskrat house. They favor the lee side of an island or the end of a peninsula adjacent to deep water. Loons come and go secretly by swimming beneath the water surface to reach the nest.

When the female lays her eggs, both parents share the incubation duties for some twenty-eight days until the eggs hatch. As soon as the chicks' black down is dry and fluffy, the parents nudge the chicks into the water, swimming with them to find a quiet, secluded cove that will serve as the family nursery.

For a short while the baby loons are allowed to ride on their parent's backs nestled on top between their wings. The chicks depend on their parents for food for three months until they develop their own fishing skills.

After it grows up, a loon is marvelously built for the water. When it dives for prey, it folds its wings close to its body, pulls in its powerful legs until only its ankles and feet protrude, and twists and turns in the water as it intercepts a fish. Heavy bones that are not honeycombed with air sacs as are the bones of most birds equip the loon to be an agile diver and strong swimmer, but not a proficient flier. Because of its weight, it is difficult for the loon to lift off the surface to fly.

Its eyes are well developed for seeing underwater. When swimming on the surface, a loon will slightly submerge its head and slowly turn it from side to side, looking deep into the water. When it sights its quarry, the head goes underwater first, followed smoothly by the rest of its body.

Although the loon is a water bird, it is not classified as a waterfowl such as a duck, goose, or swan. A number of differences in its skeleton and muscle structure set it apart, among them the fact that a loon, unlike waterfowl, walks awkwardly on land because its legs are so far back on its body.

"Around dusk on a quiet night you might hear a loon's yodeling cry," Bill advised us. Loons have a remarkable ability to vocalize; they seem to communicate with each other using four basic sounds: hoots, wails, tremolos, and yodels. Each call reflects a different message, from a desire to mate to an emergency danger signal.

All eyes swung shoreward when Bill announced he had spotted a bald eagle atop a dead pine tree. "Finding food is hard work for a predator," he said, "and an eagle is no exception. It succeeds in getting a fish only about once every ten times. It's a lot easier to find a dead fish or small animal along the shore than to rely on a live catch."

The birds we had seen, Bill remarked, were only a small portion of the rich animal life in the park. Resource management rangers estimate that Voyageurs harbors some one hundred and fifty to two hundred black bears, forty to one hundred moose, hundreds of white-tailed deer, and an estimated three thousand beavers, not to mention otter, red fox, porcupine, and coyote. Even the rare pine marten, fisher, lynx, and gray wolf live within the park. About twelve to fourteen hundred wolves live in northern Minnesota, Wisconsin, and Michigan, one of only two groups known to exist in the wild in the lower forty-eight states.

wild rice

Wild Rice

We experienced another side of the park when we signed up at the Rainy Lake visitor center for a paddle in a north canoe, a replica of the birchbark canoes used by the French-Canadian *voyageurs* (travelers) who made their living as fur trappers on this watery frontier.

Our guides, Ranger Bill Glover and park volunteers Maurice and Bea Parkin, steered us into a stand of wild rice that grew at the shallow edge of the lake. Wild rice, Maurice said, is actually not a form of rice at all but a cereal grain that grows as an aquatic grass. Like other aquatic grasses, wild rice has a hollow stem with partitions between the nodes on the stem.

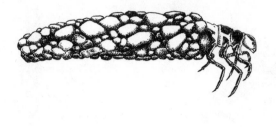

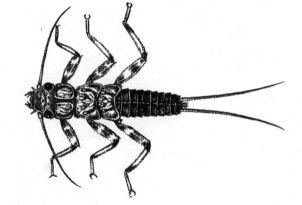

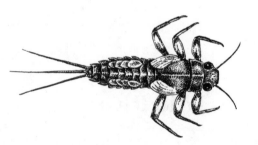

from top: caddisfly, stonefly, mayfly, leech

Since wild rice is an annual grass, it must reseed itself each year. In the spring, after winter dormancy, the seed germinates underwater, producing a single root and leaf. As more leaves sprout, the tops float up to the water surface.

By late August the rice stalks have grown four to eight feet tall. The grain ripens from the top down and if left to itself would drop into the water to provide seeds for the next year's crop.

For many years Indians in Minnesota have harvested the wild rice for food and continue to do so today. Indians retain the privilege of harvesting all the wild rice on their reservations and on all federal and state lands. They do it in the traditional manner. Two people man a small boat. One person uses two sticks to bend the rice stalk over the boat, then taps the head gently to knock off the rice grains. He leaves unripe grains untouched. The pair then repeats the process three or four times at several-day intervals to get the later ripening grains. Wild rice, a popular delicacy throughout the country, is high in protein, potassium, phosphorus, and vitamin B.

Aquatic Flies

Once or twice a week Voyageurs National Park schedules a "Kids Explore" program. We joined seasonal ranger Mary Nordeen as she and twelve children armed with dip nets, strainers, tweezers, and plastic bowls discovered the "critters" in a nearby grassy pond. Squinting to get a better sight of the aquatic insects, we learned about their immature stages—nymphs, larvae, and pupae, all of them important in the food webs of streams, ponds, and lakes. As adults, insects have three body regions: head, thorax, and abdomen. Their thorax includes three pairs of jointed legs and usually two pairs of wings.

A girl produced a tiny, pebbly object—a caddisfly larva, Mary said. The caddisfly larva encases itself in a sheath of tiny grains of sand to protect itself from being eaten before it can hatch. After seeing stoneflies, caddisflies, and mayflies in the different life stages, it was time to see some larger aquatic species.

Crayfish, mussels, leeches, and other aquatic life end up in the dip nets used by youngsters at Voyageurs National Park. Ranger Mary Nordeen identifies the trophies as the kids bring them to the surface.

Leeches

Ready for more adventure, we climbed aboard a diesel-powered "duck," a Park Service boat that has clamshell doors in the bow that open when the craft noses up on a beach. This converted World War II landing craft took us to explore nearby Squaw Frank Island.

Soon kids in soggy sneakers and wet to the knees were prowling the grassy edges of the lake as they found new "critters" like water boatmen. These slender bugs have long hind legs flattened for swimming and a beak for sucking. They feed on algae or on decaying plants from the bottom.

The biggest discovery of the day, however, was leeches—the flattened segmented worms that are abundant in calm, shallow, warm waters where the bottom is cluttered with debris. The leeches brought back to Mary were four to five inches long and dark green in color, almost black, a hue that helps these graceful-looking worms blend with the bottom vegetation where they spend part of their life. Of some forty species of leeches in the United States, only about half a dozen attach themselves to humans. Many are parasites on fish, frogs, and turtles, and some fasten themselves to snails.

Most leeches are good swimmers, their bodies making muscular ripples to help them undulate along. A leech can also move along the lake bottom by "looping," attaching first a sucker at one end of its body, then a sucker at the other end, as it loops along end over end. One common leech, the fish leech, uses its suckers to attach itself to a fish swimming by. When the fish comes close, the leech extends its unattached end until it makes contact with the fish, then lets go with the other end as it attaches itself to its new host.

After it finds its new home, the leech presses its round mouth against the skin of its host. With its small teeth it makes an incision that looks like a three-rayed star. It then sucks blood from the fish or frog, often weakening its victim. A leech can survive for as long as a year on one of these blood meals. Other kinds of leeches are scavengers and carnivores, feeding on smaller worms or food particles.

Although it is a primitive animal, a leech has a sense of sight. Some leeches have as many as ten pairs of eyes arranged in a circle at the leech's head. Using its eyes, scientists believe, it can probably detect the passing shadow of a fish swimming by.

After an hour on the beach Mary and her budding biologists hopped aboard the landing craft, each excitedly talking about the discoveries he or she had made at the water's edge; how so many living organisms can be found in a dishpan of water; and how dependent animals are on their food chain. Finally, Mary had her youthful adventurers check each other to be sure that none had become an unintended host for one of the leeches they were studying.

CHAPTER
6

Desert Southwest

RIVERS

Few rivers make their way across the sagebrush-covered expanses of the desert Southwest. This region of plateaus and basins interspersed with low mountains is the driest part of the United States.

The Pacific mountain ranges that lie close to the west coast—the Sierra Nevada, the Cascade Range, and the Coastal Range—wring most of the moisture out of the passing rain clouds, leaving little precipitation to fall on these dry inland plateaus. The few streams that do exist rarely reach the sea; they lead instead into brackish lakes such as the Great Salt Lake, are used extensively for irrigation, have their water piped to distant cities, or disappear entirely in desert sinks. Only an occasional desert thunderstorm replenishes these meager waterways. A sudden cloudburst can quickly fill a dry gulch, transforming it into a raging torrent and turning a dry area into a flood zone.

Two major rivers flow through this semiarid region: the Rio Grande and the Colorado. Both originate in the snowfields of the Rocky Mountains. Over thousands of years they have carved their way southward across the plateaus, the Rio Grande to the Gulf of Mexico, the Colorado to the Gulf of California.

The Rio Grande, the sixth longest river in North America, is 1,885 miles long. Along its upper course it bisects the state of New Mexico as it flows through a series of basins separated by narrow valleys, then widens out north of Albuquerque to flow out on a dry plateau, and finally forms the border between Texas and Mexico. The Colorado River rises close to the source of the Rio Grande, then flows southwestward, twisting for 1,450 miles as it finds its way through the southern Rocky Mountains and the Grand Canyon to Lake Mead, and finally forms the border between Arizona and California.

Water, of course, is a prized resource in the desert Southwest. To meet man's needs, both rivers are interrupted at several places by dams that create reservoirs used for power generation, water supply, irrigation, and industry. As cities grow and desert regions attract more people, the need for water increases.

During the summer the Rio Grande has been known to run dry because of lack of rainfall and the withdrawal of water for irrigation. According to laws long on the books, neighboring states have the right to withdraw water from the rivers. For example, Phoenix and Los Angeles vie with other cities, with ranchers, and with Mexico for a share of the water from the Colorado River.

Two portions of the Rio Grande have been designated as wild and scenic. The first, a forty-eight-mile segment of the upstream part of the river in New Mexico, has carved its way hundreds of feet into the plateau where its swiftly running current continues to cut its way ever deeper into ancient lava flows that once covered the landscape. The second segment is far to the south where the Rio Grande forms the border between Texas and Mexico; here a second wild section runs 250 miles through spectacular canyons and across the desert as it winds through Big Bend National Park.

We had an opportunity to explore the deep gorge of the northern segment in New Mexico when we hiked down a zigzag trail into a canyon eight hundred feet deep at the Wild Rivers Recreation Area near Taos. Our guide was a river ranger named Eileen Weidner.

Piñon Pine

The trail offered an unusual ecological experience, one you are unlikely to see elsewhere. "As we go down the slope," Eileen alerted us, "you'll see an inverted ecological pattern. Plants grow here in life zones that are reversed from their normal order."

From the plateau with its sagebrush and juniper bushes we headed down the trail. As we reached narrow benches of terrain that stairstepped down the canyon sides we observed piñon pine mixed with cottonwood trees. The piñon, she said, was in its normal habitat—piñons grow on mesa tops or mountainsides where their sweet nuts are a favorite of wildlife. Indians, too, collect them to eat or grind into flour. The piñon tree is a sturdy-looking tree and has a deep brown bark. A slow grower, it takes 250 years to reach a height of only twenty feet.

Cottonwood

The cottonwoods were out of place however. This familiar member of the willow family is a large tree that has a pale bark and a triangular leaf. Normally it is found not on the side of a canyon but on lower ground, often along a watercourse or arroyo (a dry wash). Sure enough, the cottonwoods here had found a water source on the flanks of the canyon—springs and seeps that emerged from between the rock layers.

Ponderosa Pine

At the bottom of the canyon grew yet another ecological surprise: ponderosa pine and Douglas fir. Both trees are usually found at higher elevations. The ponderosa is easy to recognize with its rough, furrowed, reddish bark and tall, straight trunk. Ponderosas often grow to 150 feet in height and three to four feet in diameter. You can identify it from its sets of three long needles. Its brown cones, three to five inches long, have spiked scales that can prick your finger. There is another way to recognize a ponderosa: find a tree that has deep cracks in its bark, preferably on the side that gets the most sun; smell the cracked area and you will detect an odor like vanilla.

Douglas Fir

This relative of the spruce also grows straight and tall, making it a much-desired tree for lumbermen. Next to the giant sequoias, the Douglas fir is the country's tallest tree, sometimes reaching three hundred feet. You can recognize its cone by the distinctive "mouse tails" that stick out from between the cone scales.

Vestiges of Thermal Activity

On our hike to the river we also learned how you can read the geological history of a canyon from its walls. Eileen pointed out the different rock layers along the trail. Layers of gravel rubble alternated with layers of black basalt, the rock that formed from the lava that had at one time covered this landscape. The river, cutting through these layers, had exposed this geological cross section to view.

She put her finger on "frozen bubbles," called vesicles, in a layer of basalt, bubbles that originally came from gas that was trapped in the molten lava as it gushed to the surface millions of years ago. With our fingers we could feel the rounded depressions frozen in the rock. The bubbles were smaller at the bottom of each layer than at the top, indicating that they had been expanding in size as they floated toward the top of the lava before the entire flow solidified into rock. Each layer of bubbles, she explained, identifies a new lava flow.

Near the canyon bottom we came across warm springs that flowed out from between rock layers, adding to the volume of water in the river. The water was warm to our touch. A hot spring results when surface water seeps deep below ground and collects in an underground pool close to molten magma, the fiery core material beneath the earth's crust. The water is heated by the magma until it boils and forces its way back to the surface where it escapes as a hot spring.

At Bandelier National Monument, which lies along a tributary of the Rio Grande south of Taos, New Mexico, we saw other evidence of ancient lava flows. This national park preserves the remains of an early cliff-dwelling settlement of the Anasazi Indians who lived there between 1150 and 1550 A.D.

As we walked a trail through the canyon ranger Rory Gauthier pointed out jagged cliffs of basaltic rock, the crystallized lava that once poured red hot and liquid from an erupting volcano. Basalt is hard, dense, and usually dark colored. The Anasazi turned the dark rock into useful implements, chipping and carving it into tools like a *mano* or a *metate*, the traditional pair of implements used by Indian women to grind corn and seeds into flour.

Rory showed us another volcanic product, obsidian, a rock even blacker and shinier than basalt. Obsidian is a natural glass that is formed when the lava cools suddenly. It contains the same elements as granite but in an uncrystallized form. To demonstrate how obsidian was used by the Indians, Rory taught himself to make arrowheads and spear points by chipping the rock to a sharp point using the tip of a deer antler.

Much of the canyon where we walked was flanked by pinkish tan cliffs that contrasted with the dark basalt. This was tuff, a much less dense and lighter weight rock that resulted from the fallout of ash that covered the volcanic region. Tuff is porous and relatively soft. Some chunks, in fact, are so light you can pick up a large stone and toss it aside. Running water quickly erodes a tuff surface, creating deep, steep-walled canyons like the one at Bandelier.

We also saw signs in the canyon walls of maar volcanic action. A maar volcano, Rory explained, is a volcano that repeatedly erupts from beneath the water of a stream or lake. Molten rock coming up and meeting the water causes steam explosions; rock fragments are thrown out and deposited on the surrounding landscape in layers. These explosions, which took place about a million years ago, occurred ten to twenty times per minute, leaving layers of different colored rock that you can still see today.

Juniper

As the trail led downward we shifted our attention from the underlying geology to the vegetation and wildlife typical of a desert canyon. Rory pointed out the one-seed juniper, a thick-stemmed bush common in much of New Mexico and Arizona. Its dark blue berries are bitter to the taste, although a number of birds and animals apparently find them delicious. The juniper, he said, is one of the most widely distributed woody plants in the world, growing throughout the northern hemisphere.

The leaves of the juniper may be needlelike and prickly or they may be scalelike and lie tightly against the twigs. Some desert varieties grow as shrubs close to the ground; other species grow to be trees many feet high. Locally, juniper trees are often referred to as cedars or red cedars, but this is misleading— they are members of the cypress family, not the pine family.

Junipers have fragrant, berrylike cones or fruits. Usually the male and female flowers grow on different trees. Only those trees that have female flowers bear fruit. The Indians learned many uses for juniper bark: they used it for sandals, roof thatching, even for baby diapers.

Yucca

To one side, growing on a steep rocky slope, was a Spanish bayonet, one of several varieties of yucca found in the canyon. It deserves its name: it is a low-growing plant that sends up sharp, spiky leaves. All yuccas have sharp, pointed leaves that protrude upward from a central stem. The leaves are often stiff and narrow and have a sawlike or fibrous edge. An evergreen, the yucca does not shed its leaves. Its flowers—usually whitish green or cream colored—grow in a cluster on a stem that springs from the center of the cluster of leaves.

"Yucca served the Indians well," Rory said. "They ate its fruit either fresh or cooked; made rope, sandals, mats, and baskets from its leaves; made soap and shampoo from its roots and stems; and even used its fibers and the sharp tips of its leaves as needle and thread." An Indian woman, he continued, could weave a yucca basket so tightly that if the basket were sealed with pitch, it would hold water and become a portable and unbreakable pot.

Ephedra

Rory bent over a low shrub whose jointed stems grew in broom-like clusters but seemed to have no true leaves. The stalks were light green in color and hollow. "This is the ephedra shrub," he said, "also known as Mormon tea." He described the interesting quality of the shrub the Indians recognized—it relieves coughing. They brewed its branches with water to produce a cough medicine. Even today commercial cough drops and cough syrups contain ephedrine.

Box Elder

The trail continued downward, skirting two high waterfalls whose drops interrupted the steady progress of the creek. Below the falls the trail moved closer to the stream bank where cotton-wood and box elder trees grew. Indians tapped the box elder for its sweetish sap, which they boiled to make a syrup similar to maple syrup.

The box elder is neither a boxwood nor an elder—it is a member of the maple family. Its leaf consists of three coarsely toothed leaflets instead of the single leaf of the maple, but its double-winged seeds identify it with the maple family. The box elder has a short trunk, wide-spreading branches, and a rounded crown. It sometimes grows up to fifty feet high but is more often a shrub of ten to fifteen feet. Because of its brittle wood it is subject to damage during wind and snowstorms and is relatively short lived.

beaver

Beaver

At the edge of a creek we came across signs of beaver activity. A beaver had gnawed halfway through the trunk of a cottonwood tree a foot in diameter. A number of stumps showed the conical shape typical of the work of this animal that combines the traits of lumberjack and engineer.

Any running waterway may get a beaver's attention, particularly a stream where there are good stands of aspen, willow, or birch trees close to the water. The beaver starts a new dam by anchoring a small stick in the stream bed, then carrying and pushing more sticks and branches to the site, arranging them into an interwoven heap. The busy aquatic engineer fills in the chinks between the sticks with mud.

The jumble of sticks also serves as the beaver's winter food supply. We saw where the rodents had cut down trees, gnawed them into lengths and dragged them to the pile. When the cold weather or snow makes it harder for the animal to get around and fringes the shore with ice, the beaver simply swims underwater to its cache of logs and stocks and selects a tasty one for lunch.

Beavers spend most of their time in the water. When swimming, a beaver generally submerges for two or three minutes at a time, although it can remain underwater for up to fifteen minutes and can travel up to half a mile if it senses danger. It swims with its webbed hind feet in unison when cruising, but switches to a powerful alternating stroke that pushes it along at about five miles an hour to get out of harm's way.

River beavers, we learned, have a tougher time of it than do beavers who live on a placid lake. A beaver that lives on a river has to cope with the rise and fall of the water level. So instead of the neat, cone-shaped lodge of the lakeside beaver, the river beaver tunnels beneath a mass of sticks and logs and builds its nest within the pile and into the riverbank. A beaver might have to build several lodges between spring and fall as the water level fluctuates. If the water level falls, it may uncover the beaver's hidden underwater entrance, exposing it to predators such as the river otter.

Beavers construct a tunnel entrance to their den that leads in below the water surface, then inclines upward within the riverbank, ending in a hollowed-out nest chamber. If the beaver has excavated the shaft high enough, the crest of the water at flood stage will not rise to the level of the nest. If it does, the beaver family must swim out of their flooded home and abandon the site.

The work of the beaver can readily change the environment. As a pond backs up behind the dam, the water covers the bases of nearby trees, causing them to die and collapse. Fish, ducks, waterfowl, and amphibians find a new home. Raccoons, ospreys, hawks, owls, and other predators arrive, attracted by the new possibilities for prey.

Ranger Rory Gauthier examines the handiwork of an ambitious beaver near a stream that runs through Bandelier National Monument. Another night's work with its sharp teeth and this cottonwood will topple.

To spot a beaver dam along a riverbank, look for several clues. The pile of saplings at the entrance, of course, is a good sign. Other clues to look for are a number of trees nearby that have been cut by the beaver's sharp teeth (note the cone shape cut on the remaining stump) and well-marked trails that lead from the river back into thickets and woods near the river.

To view the beaver at work in a river or lake setting, Rory counseled, come back to the scene of activity at dusk or on a cloudy day. Find a good place nearby where you cannot readily be seen and observe quietly. If you are fortunate, you will see the beaver waddle up on land, stand on its hind legs as it gnaws its way through a tree trunk with its four large incisor teeth, and drag its prize to the creek bank. After cutting the trunk or

A partially completed beaver dam draws the attention of ranger Linda Bishop on a tributary of the Buffalo River. The animal had done this much in only a few days' time, since the dam had not been there a week before. The best time to see a beaver in action is at dusk when it leaves its den to go to work.

branches into smaller pieces, the beaver pulls each branch through the water to add to its dam.

Mule Deer

Hiking on down the trail, we suddenly saw a bush move. Peering carefully in that direction, we spotted a doe mule deer, half hidden behind some bushes, busily browsing. We identified it by its large, upright ears and confirmed our sighting when the deer turned and we could see its white rump and black-tipped tail.

Had we startled it, we might have noted another identifying trademark—the odd, stiff-legged bounding gait the mule deer

mule deer

uses to escape from danger. In this technique called "stotting," so different from the normal bounding action of its eastern cousin, the white-tailed deer, the mule deer lands on all four feet at the same time. It can even turn its entire body in the opposite direction during a single bound.

The variety of trees and shrubs in the canyon, Rory said, as well as the water available in the creek, make this an ideal habitat for deer. Although mule deer are primarily browsers, they may graze on grass and new growth in the spring in order to build up their body fat after the lean winter. Traveling in search of new food sources is no problem for the mule deer. Seasonal migrations of many miles from summer ranges in the high country to lowland winter ranges are a common occurrence.

Mule deer remain abundant in the arid terrain of the West; biologists estimate that some four million live there. Mule deer are capable of living in remarkably different types of habitat ranging from alpine meadow to desert scrub, arid plain, prairie, chap-

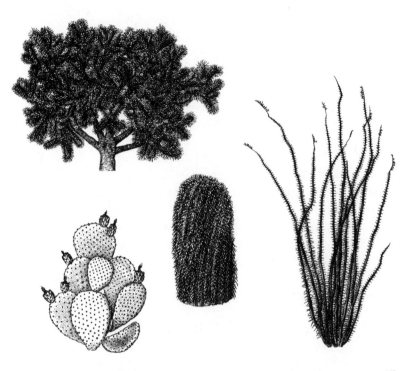

top: cholla cactus; bottom, left to right: prickly pear, barrel cactus, ocotillo

paral, woodland, boreal mountain, and temperate and tropical coniferous forest.

With such a wide distribution, your chances of observing a mule deer in a river or lake environment are excellent. Look for them in the early morning and from dusk to several hours after dark. Mule deer like to browse among shrubs where their tawny color helps them blend with the scenery or along the edge of a forest or other high growth that provides them a handy escape route.

Canyon Geology

Like an elongated doughnut, our large pontoon raft slid downstream, borne by the powerful Colorado River as it twisted through the awe-inspiring Grand Canyon.

For six action-packed days nineteen of us led by a crew of three thrilled as we covered 225 miles, hurtled through more than a hundred rapids, gazed up at the canyon's multicolored rock flanks, and camped out at night on some of the few sandy beaches that spread a welcome mat for rafters along the river's edge.

For Marge and me it was the fulfillment of a life's ambition to float this scenic route through the Grand Canyon, and we had signed up for the trip six months ahead of time. Now here we were getting a firm grip on one of the raft's handholds as we lunged into a rapid, riding the raft as you would a bronco as the spray whipped into our faces.

Rafting a river, we found, is a great leveler. Corporate presidents and plumbers all get soaked by the same waves and gaze at the same wildflowers cascading down craggy hillsides. People of all ages, sexes, and backgrounds feel the same fear and anticipation at approaching an awesome-looking rapid. Successfully negotiating one, like living through any frightening experience, brings an exhilaration and quiet self-respect in having felt fear and overcome it.

Rafting the Colorado is also an expedition through the depths of a canyon more than a mile deep where the only other way in or out for people or animals is through an occasional side canyon. Millions of people annually view the Grand Canyon from its rim, but only some twenty thousand a year get to observe the natural history of the river and its gorge from the water level.

The Colorado River drops ten thousand feet over hundreds of rapids in its descent from the Rocky Mountains in Colorado to the Gulf of California. Over the years the river currents have etched deep canyons into the high plateaus. Rushing currents of the river, especially when the river is flooding, pick up and carry along tons of sand and rock fragments. These particles and pieces bombard the bedrock of the river bottom and banks, acting like an ever-moving strip of sandpaper as they bite deeper and deeper into the bottom. Studies show that over the last thousand years the bottom of the Colorado River has dropped six and one-half inches due to this wearing action. In recent years, however, this cutting action of the river has been slowed by the construction of two dams on the main stem (the Hoover Dam and the Glen Canyon Dam) and by other dams on its tributaries.

In its cutting, the river is like a giant knife that slices through a layer cake—the cake being the various rock strata that have been laid down on top of one another. As you float through the

Grand Canyon, and down many another western river as well, it's like reading a geology textbook. The history of the formation of the earth is written in the layers of the canyon walls.

As we drifted downstream through the depths of this great gash our leader, Ron Thompson, explained how the different rock layers reflected their origins. Millions of years ago, he said, large seas covered the land, laying down sediments that later hardened into rocks such as limestone, sandstone, and shale. Later, entire sections of the earth's crust were uplifted by forces beneath the surface. Rocks that were formed as marine sediment were now raised so that many of them protruded thousands of feet above sea level. Such rocks are called *sedimentary*.

It is the sedimentary rocks that add most of the color to the Grand Canyon, as well as to other canyons on the Southwest. We found their color an important indicator of which kind of rock we were passing. The buff of a sandstone is a result of the sand from which it is made; the gray, red, and green of shale and the gray, white and red of limestone testify to their beginnings. Hermit shale, for example, is red, the result of iron compounds in the mud and clay from which it formed. A white limestone reflects its origin as a marine reef that was once made up of millions of tiny coral animals with whitish shells. You sometimes even see wavy lines from the sea or fossils of marine plants and animals in sedimentary rocks.

Nevertheless, geologists caution about identifying rocks by their color alone, because rocks can change color due to staining. Redwall limestone, for example, is actually a whitish rock that gets its red color from iron oxides that leach out of a layer of hermit shale that often lies above it.

A second type of rock, *igneous* rock, is generally darker in color. These are much older rocks, chunks of lava and cinders that were disgorged from volcanoes or rocks formed in the molten interior of the earth and brought to the surface. We soon learned to identify the dark gray of the basalt. Igneous rocks are much harder than sedimentary rocks and therefore more resistant to erosion.

A third kind of rock is called *metamorphic*. This type was formed many years ago when tremendous heat and pressure far beneath the earth's surface caused rocks below to recrystallize into new minerals, transforming their composition. Metamorphic rocks such as schist and gneiss are the hardest and oldest of the canyon rocks. Almost black, schist is sometimes worn to a smooth, shiny surface by the constant friction of the river flow and is easy to recognize. At times we saw streaks of another metamorphic rock, granite, within a formation of schist—the pink granite had been forced into the schist as an intrusion, probably the result of some fiery volcanic outburst from below.

These three types of rock, each formed in a different way, have also been molded and shaped by surface effects that have acted upon them. Water, wind, and ice have all played a role. As we floated along we saw how water from the flowing river has smoothed the canyon walls; how wind has eroded the softer sandstone rock; how "grinders," or small rocks, have been caught in a pocket and have been spun by the rushing water, drilling holes into the rock face; how rainwater has collected in fissures, frozen, then expanded to crack off large rock slabs.

Another surface effect that is common on many a canyon wall in the Southwest is "desert varnish," a black high-gloss discoloration that spreads like a curtain over a rock face. Scientists have found that desert varnish is the result of fine clay, carried by the wind, that is deposited on the rocks. Manganese and iron oxides that are leached out of the rocks by falling rain interact with the film of clay to create the dark draperies.

The clay and oxides depend on one another. The clay particles, which are dry and fluffy, depend on the oxides to hold the particles to the rocks. The oxides bridge across the clay particles and cement them, keeping the clay particles from blowing off in the next windstorm.

The ancient inhabitants of the desert made use of this discoloration on the rocks as a good place to carve symbolic pictures called *petroglyphs*. They scratched their designs into the rock, exposing the tan and gray stone beneath the dark overlay of desert varnish.

The geology lesson continued with Ron describing each new layer as we floated through the canyon's unparalleled mingling of rocks of different ages. We learned to appreciate one rock type in particular the day we were searching for a campsite during threatening weather. Ron guided the raft into a small beach that backed up to a rock wall of brownish Tapeats sandstone that has shalelike layers. By its nature Tapeats has broad ledges and overhangs—just the thing for weary rafters seeking to pitch their tents and spread out their sleeping bags in a dry spot. We were

A swimmer splashes in a warm pool while the cooler Colorado River (42 degrees) flows by. Travertine pools like these within the Grand Canyon are warmed by volcanic activity beneath the surface.

even more delighted to have found these overhangs when it rained later that night.

"That's why we call the Tapeats 'the friendly rock layer'," said Chuck Boebinger, another of our guides, over breakfast the next morning. "You found shelter under it the same way the Indians in the canyon have for many years."

Several times during our journey Ron nosed the big raft into the bank and invited everyone ashore to explore a side canyon. These branch canyons, which often hold surprises waiting to be discovered, are formed by water runoff from the canyon rim as it cuts its way down to the river. Rock slides and weathering also help shape each side canyon.

One warm afternoon Chuck led us along a narrow trail that clung to the steep flanks of Havasu Creek, a side canyon stream whose waters were a brilliant turquoise from the high calcium carbonate content, in contrast to the dark blue of the Colorado itself. After crossing and recrossing the stream several times, we reached a pool where the water pours over layers of travertine, a crust of minerals that has precipitated out of these calcium-rich waters to form a series of natural steps beneath a waterfall.

Canyon Vegetation

Vegetation along the canyon is just as fascinating as the geology. The variety is remarkable—no less than five of the seven life zones of North America are represented in the canyon environment, zones that range from subalpine to desert. A person would have to travel from northern Canada to Mexico to pass through as many climatic zones. As you move downstream through these life zones, a forest of ponderosa pine, Douglas fir, and aspen of the high country gives way to twisted piñon and juniper pines, then finally to the tropical desert growth of agave, blackbrush, and prickly pear cactus.

Each plant, animal, or fish, Ron reminded us, occupies a special role that affects, and is affected by, its environment. This role is called its ecological niche. For example, some plants succeed in growing even in a tiny crevice in a rock wall. Winds blow soil into the crevice and rains provide water. Seeds and spores land on the spot; some of them find a suitable home, sprout, and grow, and in their living improve the environment so that other plants can flourish. Narrowleaf yucca can take root in even a small crevice like this, growing into a plant with spiky leaves and a single tall shaft of flowers.

The narrowleaf yucca also illustrates the interdependence between some plants and insects, in this case the yucca moth. The yucca plant and the moth need each other. When the yucca is in flower, the moth flies from flower to flower, carrying pollen from one to the other, thus fertilizing the yuccas and insuring their reproduction.

But the moth depends just as much on the yucca and cannot reproduce without it. As the moth flits between the flowers the female lays her eggs within one of them. When the moth larvae hatch, they feed on the seeds of the flower, developing and growing into a new generation of moths that will repeat the process.

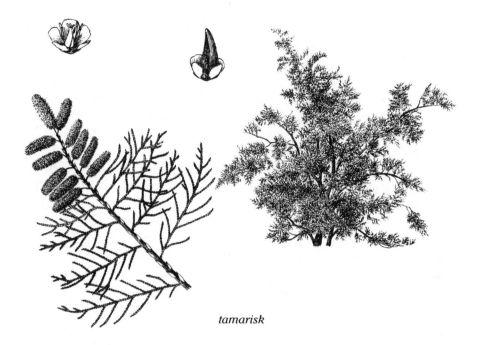

tamarisk

In the upper canyon Ron called our attention to shadscale bushes, Mormon tea, and the century plant with its single straight spike of flowers. He also pointed out two kinds of cactus. The hedgehog cactus resembles its namesake animal with long, sharp bristles that effectively ward off wildlife seeking to take a bite out of it. It grows in a clump with fat, round stems that rise twelve to fifteen inches high. The purplish pink flowers in the spring develop into fruits that taste like strawberries.

Prickly pear cacti, which are found throughout the canyon, have flat, fleshy stems covered with barbed hairs. This cactus grows in sprawling clumps up to a foot high although prickly pear varieties growing elsewhere sometimes reach tree height. Springtime endows the cactus with a yellow flower with a reddish center that precedes a spineless red fruit that is a favorite of wood rats and other rodents.

In the middle canyon other desert plants added a splotch of green to the gray, rocky slopes of *talus*, the rock debris that falls to the base of a cliff. Brickelbush, a waist-high shrub, blooms with small yellow flowers; its triangular leaf gives off an aromatic smell when crushed. Goldenweed, a stalky shrub of similar height, has leaves that are sticky to the touch and smell like turpentine. The fishhook cactus, named for the hooked spikes that cover its cylindrical stems, flourishes in the shade of larger plants and bushes.

In the lower canyon that extends through the hot Mojave Desert you find several other kinds of cactus that underline the diversity of this plant family. The teddy bear cholla lives up to its lighthearted name with plump segmented stems connected by joints. The massive barrel cactus grows to fully nine feet in height and two feet in diameter; it can absorb so much water after a cloudburst that it will topple over. The ocotillo cactus has an entirely different appearance: long feathery branches that sweep upward from its base to a height of six feet or more.

Creosote bush, the dark green bush that frequently dots open expanses of desert shrubland, also grows in the canyon. It grows five to eight feet high, shoots its branches upward in a spray from its base, and produces a resin that smells like balsam.

Canyon Fish

Fish in the river also find their appropriate ecological niche. When man intruded and built the Glen Canyon Dam in 1963 for electric power generation and water storage, the fish life underwent a change. Prior to the dam, water temperatures in the river fluctuated between freezing during the winter to eighty degrees Fahrenheit in the summer. Today the water temperatures stay consistently below fifty degrees year round. This is because the water released from Lake Powell, the lake impounded by the dam, comes from the cold bottom layer of the lake where sunshine cannot warm it.

As a result, the river water is too chilly for humans to swim in and apparently too cold for such indigenous fish as the Colorado River squawfish, humpback chub, and razorback sucker to spawn in. The cold water, however, suits rainbow, brook, and brown trout. The trout, which were introduced as game species, thrive in clear, cold water. The squawfish and other varieties, unable to find their niche in a changed environment, may soon be extinct.

Ranger Anne Apodaca of the Bureau of Land Management holds a handful of branches of the tamarisk, a shrub that grows along many of the rivers of the Southwest. In the winter the tamarisk loses its leaves and turns a reddish color; in the spring it leafs out and turns green.

Tamarisk

The dam has brought changes in riverside vegetation as well. When the river ran free, an average of 380,000 tons of silt came down the river every day, much of it deposited along the way on shoreline beaches. Now most of the silt is held back by the dam, allowing only some 40,000 tons a day to drift down the river. The river no longer deposits new layers of sand on the beaches; instead, the currents are slowly eroding away the beaches that are there.

In earlier days heavy spring floods, unrestrained by a dam, scoured the riverbanks, carrying away many of the plants that had gained a foothold during the growing season. Now, with no such flushing action in the spring, plants continue to flourish and grow.

"What's happened," Ron said, "is that we're seeing a whole new fringe of green growth along the river's edge. That might be fine except a lot of that green growth is tamarisk—and that's a problem."

Tamarisk, he explained, spreads rapidly, crowding out other species such as willows, cottonwoods, and mesquites. The tamarisk drips sap onto the ground where it grows, in effect poisoning the soil so that the seeds of other plants cannot sprout. Tamarisks, sometimes called salt cedars, are feathery-looking bushes that grow to fifteen to twenty feet in height. They have wispy branches and small leaves. Tamarisk is gray-green in color during the growing season but forms a fringe of dark red stalks along the river during the winter.

The tamarisk has two other characteristics that have made it unpopular throughout the Southwest. It is a particularly thirsty plant and is a poor source of food and shelter for wildlife. One large tamarisk can absorb as much as two hundred gallons of water a day, about the amount used per day by a small family. This heavy uptake robs a river like the Colorado or Rio Grande of water that could nourish other vegetation or be used to irrigate crops.

Nevertheless, the increase in vegetation along the river as a result of the dam does provide additional food and cover for wildlife. Mule deer forage at the riverside and coyotes and bobcats roam the canyon, effectively holding down the thriving jackrabbit and rodent populations.

Desert Bighorn Sheep

One day, as we rounded an outcropping of rock in our raft, we surprised several desert bighorn sheep as they browsed on the sparse shrubs of a rocky slope leading down to the river. With their gray-brown coats they blended almost perfectly with the jumble of sandstone boulders. "It's great to find the sheep so close to the water," enthused Ron. "Usually they're farther up the slope."

Ron steered the big pontoon out of the current and into an eddy, holding it with his outboard motor from drifting downstream so that all hands could get a good look at the sheep. A ram, three ewes, and a lamb nibbled on some acacia bushes and other low shrubs. The ram stood aloof, as if on sentinel duty. The

desert bighorn

lamb stayed close to its mother while the others jumped easily from rock to rock to sample different bushes.

Desert bighorns also feed on willow, mountain mahogany, desert holly, Russian thistle, and prickly pear cactus, eating coarse vegetation that other animals spurn. They can consume such rough vegetation because they have a complex digestive system that allows them to chew their food several times to get all the nutrients from it.

A canyon like the Colorado's provides a good habitat for bighorn sheep, which need to drink water at least every two or three days to stay healthy. A sheep loses body weight quickly if denied water. Within minutes after drinking, the bighorn seems to revive, perking up and appearing trim and strong once again.

Ron said he was sure the sheep had seen us for they have excellent eyesight. Sharp vision, more than their hearing or sense of smell, warns bighorn sheep of intruders.

The rocky habitat that the sheep favor provides the bighorn with its main defense. If threatened, it simply bounds away up the rocks, easily outdistancing a predator that is not as surefooted. Their ability to leap smoothly from rock to rock derives from the remarkable structure of their hooves. The halves of each hoof are able to separate from each other, allowing the animal to cling firmly to the rockiest terrain. The sole of the hoof is soft and cushioned—"sort of like velcro," Ron said—and helps the bighorn keep its footing as it moves across uneven or slippery surfaces.

The number of desert bighorn sheep in the West has declined in the last century due to excessive hunting, disease, and the loss of rocky habitat. Now the animals are found on only a fraction of the territory where they once roamed. We counted ourselves lucky indeed to have observed this small herd browsing in an isolated part of the canyon.

Ground Squirrel

Far more common are rodents like the common ground squirrel we saw scampering over canyon boulders. Rock squirrels, one of several species of ground squirrels, inhabit the Grand Canyon. Ground squirrels are similar in appearance to chipmunks, though chipmunks generally have bushier tails. You may have to get out your field guide to identify the species of ground squirrel or chipmunk that inhabits the region where you are. The rock squirrel is ten to eleven inches long with a seven- to ten-inch tail and has grayish fur mixed with cinnamon or brown.

Although they occupy the hottest, most arid parts of the canyon, these squirrels may be seen on even the most scorching days. A ground squirrel keeps cool by foraging in the shade of rocks and shrubs for the vegetation and insects it eats, then retreating to its burrow for short rest periods. Its light fur tends to reflect the heat and it holds its tail over its back like a parasol.

Ringtail

The squirrels attract the ringtail, a cousin of the raccoon, which prowls the cliffs, valley floor, and talus slopes. The ringtail, like the raccoon, lives near the water. It is a slender brown animal with a pointed nose and gets its name from its foot-long, fluffy, black-and-white striped tail that it can arch gracefully over its head or carry straight out behind it.

Although the ringtail lives in semiarid landscapes, it is seldom far from a water source. But if drought comes to the region and streams run dry, the ringtail adapts by concentrating its urine, thereby conserving body moisture. It makes nightly forays in search of food: small mammals like ground squirrels, mice, and kangaroo rats, as well as birds, bird eggs, snakes, lizards, grasshop-

ringtail

pers, and vegetation, particularly berry seeds. The ringtail makes its den in a narrow opening high in the rocks, an opening wide enough for it to squeeze into but not wide enough to permit its enemies, the coyote and bobcat, to enter. When agitated, the ringtail gives a coughing bark similar to that of a fox.

Canyon Birds

Birds add to the variety of wildlife in the canyon. Although they are active during the day, their ability to fly allows them to escape the heat. A bird can always fly to the cool river to get a drink or a bath, migrate upslope if the day is hot, or ride a thermal air current to an altitude where the air is cooler.

As we drifted slowly across a quiet pool between rapids we were intrigued by the swooping, darting flight of squadrons of violet-green swallows as they whirled over our heads to pluck insects out of the air. The bird gets its name from the glossy green and violet feathers on its back that contrast sharply with the snow white of its breast and rump.

We could always count on the ravens, the clean-up experts of the canyon, to take care of any tidbit of food our party might have left in camp. The common raven is totally black like a crow but is four or five inches longer and weighs twice as much. A scavenger on the ground, the raven is a talented aerialist in the sky, soaring high over the canyon in lazy circles as it rides the thermal currents on motionless wings.

Observing Canyon Wildlife

In a desert canyon, where summer temperatures can reach 120 degrees Fahrenheit on the floor of the gorge, you will rarely see animals on the ground at midday. Most are nocturnal, foraging for their prey at day's end or after dark when the canyon cools. So you are better off looking for tracks or droppings that will provide clues to the animals that inhabit the area. One day we spotted the unmistakable footprints and log-skid marks left by a beaver in a mudbank; these signs indicated that the beaver had dragged a branch across the bank to reach its lodge in the riverbank.

Another day we beached our raft for a rest stop at Redwall Cavern, a huge overhanging cave that provides a natural backdrop like an outdoor stage for one of the broadest beaches within the canyon.

As we walked across the sand Ron pointed to the tracks of a kangaroo rat, a sandpiper, a lizard, and dozens of beetles and ant lions. All of them, we knew, were undoubtedly below ground in their burrows or nests at this time of day, keeping themselves cool and conserving the water in their bodies. But when the sun went down and the heat receded, these unseen creatures, along with dozens of bats that live in the caves, would venture out to make their nocturnal rounds. The world of wildlife along the river would become active once again.

LAKES

In most freshwater lakes, streams lead both into the lake and away from it, constantly replenishing the oxygen in its waters

Beaches like this along rivers of the Southwest are excellent places to look for animal tracks. This beach near Redwall Cavern in the Grand Canyon produced tracks of kangaroo rats, lizards, sandpipers, and dozens of beetles during one observation.

and helping to circulate the water. The dissolved oxygen and other elements, combined with sunlight and photosynthesis, encourage the growth of a variety of aquatic plants. The plants in turn nourish a variety of invertebrates, insects, amphibians, and fish.

In a salt lake, on the other hand, streams flow into the lake but none lead away from it. With no outlet, the lake begins to evaporate, especially in a hot, arid climate. As the water evaporates, the percentage of minerals in the lake—the salt content—increases. Every lake contains some dissolved minerals, but when the concentration of these solutes exceeds 3 percent by weight, it is classified as a salt lake. By comparison, the average salt content of the world's oceans is 3.5 percent.

Salt lakes are surprisingly common; they occupy as much of the earth's surface as do freshwater lakes. Most often salt lakes occur in the arid regions of a country. Even Antarctica, which is a desert based on its precipitation, has some salt lakes.

In the United States most salt lakes are in the western part of the country where the feeder streams are rich in mineral content and where a number of lakes have no outlet. If you put together the high mineral content of a dead-end lake and the high evaporation rate from a dry, sunny climate, you have all the ingredients for a salt lake. When the lake's water evaporates faster than it can be replenished by the inflow, the lake's salinity increases. If evaporation continues to outpace the inflow, the lake will eventually dry up and die.

The Great Salt Lake seemed like anything but a calm lake that was drying up the day that John Malmborg, superintendent of Great Salt Lake State Park in northwestern Utah, took us in the park's rescue boat out onto this huge expanse of water. Wind whipped the lake surface into a tapestry of whitecaps, piling up blobs of spindrift, the froth of salt spray, against the shoreline. Four-foot-high waves marched toward our boat in steady procession, lifting the craft's prow high in the air, then sending it crashing down atop the next wave.

As we bucked the waves John related how Great Salt Lake came to be the remnant of the huge prehistoric Lake Bonneville that once covered twenty thousand square miles in what is now Utah, Nevada, and Idaho. The basin had filled with water during the last Ice Age. Many years ago part of the huge lake drained away into the Columbia River basin to the north, but in recent times it is the combination of high evaporation and insufficient inflow that has caused the shrinkage to continue.

Today Great Salt Lake, the largest remaining part of the prehistoric lake, has dwindled to about fifteen hundred square miles in size, with an average depth of only thirteen feet. It is North America's largest and saltiest lake, saltier than all others in the world except for the Dead Sea, which lies between Israel and Jordan.

The sun shines on the shallow lake an average of 70 percent of the time and its water temperature frequently reaches ninety degrees Fahrenheit. These conditions supply enough radiant energy to evaporate almost four feet of water each year. If no water were added, the lake would dry up in a few years.

Evidence of high salt content in Great Salt Lake is its spindrift, a combination of salt and spray whipped up by winds.

But nature is rarely so straightforward. Actually, the lake expands and contracts in cycles depending on the inflow from the tributaries—the Bear, the Weber, and the Jordan rivers—that lead into the basin from the nearby Wasatch mountains. The latest cycle began in 1982 when the lake began to rise, peaking in 1986 and 1987 when a near-record high level overwashed recreational beaches, destroyed homes and businesses, flooded an important interstate highway, and disturbed the feeding pattern of thousands of migratory birds when it submerged several wildlife refuges. Then in 1988 the lake began contracting once more.

The salt content varies indirectly with the lake's size. At its present size the salt content of the two halves of the lake (it is divided into two sections by a railroad causeway) is 25 percent for the north arm where less fresh water enters and 13 percent for the south arm. That makes the lake from four to eight times as salty as the ocean.

Like other salt lakes, John explained, Great Salt Lake has no bottom vegetation and little other vegetation except salt-tolerant algae. Only where the freshwater tributaries enter the lake and the water becomes brackish can ordinary fish, birds, and mammals exist. But a few hardy species have adapted to life in the briny portion of the lake. Several species of algae, bacteria, and protozoa exist that are invisible to the eye. Some algae live on the bottom where they build rocklike accumulations that resemble coral reefs in the ocean. These bacteria and algae serve as the food source for the few forms of animal life that can survive in the salty environment. We got a close look at one of these species when John guided the boat into the still water behind a breakwater.

Brine Shrimp

As we looked over the side we saw thousands of tiny brine shrimp floating close to the water surface. The curious little creature that has adapted to this salty environment is one-quarter to one-half inch long, a fraction of the size of the familiar shrimp of the Gulf of Mexico. Its thin body sprouts twelve legs on either side and a curving tail. Depending on which tiny bacteria and algae it has been eating, it has a light reddish brown to light blue-green hue. To us, however, it appeared translucent.

To increase their numbers, brine shrimp are able to reproduce both sexually and asexually. In the summer the eggs they produce are soft-shelled and hatch within a few hours. Later in the season, however, the eggshells are hard. With the additional protection of the hard shells, the eggs can endure freezing temperatures and long periods of drought yet still hatch out when warmth and moisture return.

Because of this characteristic of the shrimp eggs, tropical fish food producers have found they can dry the hard-shelled eggs and set them aside for several years, then ship the eggs to customers who add them to their fish tanks to hatch as fish food.

During the summer the brine shrimp are so prolific you can reach your hand into shallow water near the shore and scoop up several hundred of them. When conditions are right, they swarm by the millions, producing streaks and patches on the lake. Few if any of the adults live through the cold winter months; only the hard-shelled eggs carry the species from season to season.

It is the brine shrimp, oddly enough, that are indirectly responsible for the unique round, soft sand found on the beaches around the lake. It is unlike the sand you find accumulated at places like Indiana Dunes on Lake Michigan where the sand originates from crumbled fragments of rock washed down from higher ground. Great Salt Lake sand forms in the water. Each grain begins as a small nucleus, generally a pellet cast out by the brine shrimp's digestive system. Small crystals of calcium carbonate derived from the lake water form a coating on the rounded nucleus, eventually growing large enough to be visible. Wave action smooths the grains, called oolites, and pushes them onto the shore where they create a soft, sandy beach.

Brine Fly

An insect, the brine fly, also plays an important role in the salt-lake habitat. The brine fly, which is only one-quarter the size of an ordinary house fly, begins life as a tiny egg in the salty water, passes through larval stages as it feeds on algae and bacteria, grows into a pupal stage, and hatches. Surprisingly, the fly completes this cycle of development in as little as thirty-six hours.

In the summertime brine flies swarm in uncounted millions. They hover close to the ground, never flying above knee height to a human, and do not bite or sting. They swarm in thick masses at the water's edge, creating a barrier several feet wide that anyone going into the water has to cross.

It is these multitudes of brine shrimp and brine flies that provide the main food source for the birds that find the salty environment of the lake to their liking.

California Gull

The California gull is the most prominent of these. The state bird of Utah, the gull is held in high regard and is protected by law (in 1848 gulls destroyed a plague of crickets that threatened the crops of the Mormon pioneers). These seabirds spend the winter on the Pacific coast, then fly to Great Salt Lake in March or April to lay their eggs. The gulls nest in colonies and build basinlike homes of weeds and grasses, sometimes only a foot or so from their neighbors. Should an intruder approach the colony, the whole flock of gulls will swirl up and fill the air with their squawking. They raise their young to self-sufficiency before they depart again in late September or October.

The California gull is about the same size as the common herring gull, has gray wings, a black tail, and white neck and underbody. It carries a red spot on its yellow bill. Gulls are opportunistic feeders and eat almost anything. We watched as they floated in the shallows, bobbing their bills into the water to pluck out the brine shrimp one by one. At other times a gull would run along the beach with its bill wide open, scooping up whole mouthfuls of brine flies as they hovered over the sand.

White Pelican

Another notable visitor to the lake is the American white pelican. Some ten-thousand of these totally white birds arrive each year to make their nests and hatch their eggs on an uninhabited island in the big lake.

"Gunnison Island is just right for a pelican rookery," remarked Don Paul, chief of the Non-game Wildlife Division of the Fish and Game Department. "It has a gently sloping beach that allows the birds to nest close together. What's more, the birds have no predators on the island."

Soon after their arrival the pelicans conduct courtship rituals, choosing their mates and selecting a nest site within their colony. The female normally lays two eggs two days apart sometime between late March and late June.

Since the pelican's main food is fish and fish can live only at the brackish inlets to Great Salt Lake, the pelicans must fly to nearby lakes and freshwater marshes in search of food for themselves and their young. Unlike the brown pelican, the white pelican never dives for its meal. Instead, four or five of the birds swim abreast, gliding smoothly into the shallow water of a lake, where in a curved line they thrash the water with wings spanning nine feet. Then they scoop up the startled fish that try to dart past.

Pelican pairs share the parental duties at the nest, both throughout incubation and after the young have been born. During incubation the male and female alternate sitting on the eggs for about seventy-two hours while the other flies off to forage for fish. After the babies hatch, one of the parents will head for the foraging grounds every twenty-four to forty-eight hours, returning to feed the young and to exchange places with its mate.

Phalarope

Another bird that finds a way to overcome the salty environment of the lake is Wilson's phalarope. A long-distance traveler, the phalarope comes to feast on the shrimp and flies, molt its feathers, and gain weight to prepare itself for a migration that takes it from Canada to the high Andes of South America. If it were unable to make this stopover to feed at Great Salt Lake, the phalarope could not reach its destination.

The female phalarope has brighter plumage than the male, with tricolored wings of gray, white, and cinnamon in contrast to the male's gray-brown. Both have white and black markings on the head and a white breast although the female sports a cinnamon neck stripe. The phalarope's bill is thin and much longer than its head.

Phalaropes spend most of their time feeding on the wide lake, snapping up brine shrimp in their long beaks. An estimated 500,000 phalaropes swoop into Great Salt Lake each summer to take advantage of this bonanza of fast food, then fly on to winter in Chile and Argentina.

The gulls, pelicans, and phalaropes that have adapted to the forbidding environment of this saline lake manage to support themselves on the few species that can tolerate the salty conditions. Because of a lack of competition from other birds, the shrimp and flies represent an adequate food supply. In this desert region, where rivers often run dry and lakes evaporate to become dry lake beds, finding the food they need is no small accomplishment.

CHAPTER
7

Mountainous West

RIVERS

Much of the western part of the United States lies between two mountain chains that sweep from north to south across the landscape, their crumpled geography decreeing where rivers and lakes shall exist.

The Rocky Mountains rise as an abrupt transition from the flatness of the Great Plains, extending southward from Alaska and western Canada across the western United States, finally dwindling into the deserts of New Mexico. The Pacific Mountain Range—consisting of the Cascade Range to the north, the Coastal Range, and the Sierra Nevada—lifts its numerous peaks at the country's far western edge. Between these two mountain barriers that bracket the western part of the nation stretches the Great Basin, an extensive region of high plateaus interspersed with smaller mountains and basins.

Clouds borne by the prevailing winds sweep in from the Pacific Ocean to meet first the Pacific Mountain Range, then the Rocky Mountains. Both mountain ranges deflect the winds upward. The clouds, cooling as they rise, release moisture as rain or snow that falls primarily on the mountains' western slopes.

The results of this difference in moisture fallout are often dramatically visible. Within a few miles of a mountain crest, the color of the terrain may change from green on the west to brown on the east. A western slope will be dominated by Douglas fir and western hemlock, which need heavy rainfall; the nearby eastern slope will be covered with ponderosa and other pines, which survive on only a few inches of rainfall a year.

In places within this mountain system the precipitation adds up to some of the greatest in the United States. In the northern Cascades snowfall averages 665 inches a year, even reaching a remarkable one thousand inches at some locations. Snow that does not melt and run off accumulates on the slopes as snowfields and glaciers. Some peaks remain snow-covered year round.

Many rivers are born from the rainfall and snowfall that blanket these mountains. On the Pacific coast most streams flow down the western slopes that get the most rainfall, many of them feeding into the two major rivers of the region, the Sacramento River and the San Joaquin River. The two rivers eventually join, flowing through low fertile farmland and bays, to empty into San Francisco Bay.

Inland, in the Rocky Mountain Range, rivers flow both east and west, depending on from which side of the Continental Divide they originate. The Divide, an imaginary north-south line along the crest of the Rockies, determines whether a river drains eastward toward the Mississippi River and the Gulf of Mexico or westward toward the Pacific Ocean. Major rivers that originate in the Rocky Mountains and flow eastward are the Missouri, Yellowstone, Platte, Arkansas, and Canadian rivers. Those that flow westward include the Colorado, Snake, Salmon, Clearwater, and Columbia rivers.

The Columbia River is the major river of the Pacific Northwest. It stretches for 1,214 miles, second longest of rivers in the Western hemisphere that flow into the Pacific Ocean. Only the Yukon River in Alaska and Canada is longer. The Columbia played an important role in U. S. history. Explorers Meriwether Lewis and William Clark in 1804 and 1805 followed the Snake River—the Columbia's longest tributary—then the Columbia itself to the Pacific. Later the river provided a route for thousands of settlers in covered wagons as they made their way through the mountains to the coast.

In the last sixty years the Columbia, more than any other river in North America, has been harnessed to serve man's needs. No fewer than fourteen dams have been built on the main stem of the U. S. portion of the river, including Grand Coulee, the world's number one producer of electricity. The Columbia River accounts for one-third of all the hydroelectric power generated in the nation. In 1986 Congress established the Columbia River

Gorge National Scenic Area, which enables people to pursue recreation on the river and enjoy the gorge's diversity of natural and man-made environments.

Salmon

The dams that have altered the flow of the Columbia River have also had their effect on the salmon that call the river home. Like the American shad (page 32), Pacific salmon are anadromous

chinook salmon

fish. They hatch in fresh water in the far reaches of a tributary, descend to the ocean where they attain most of their growth, then return to their native stream to spawn. A difference between shad and Pacific salmon, however, is that Pacific salmon always die after spawning.

The largest of the Pacific salmon is the chinook, which averages twenty-two pounds and sometimes attains a weight of as much as ninety pounds. This kind of salmon may travel some two thousand miles through ocean and river to spawn, refusing all food during its months-long journey. All of its energy stored from years of feeding in the ocean is diverted to producing eggs or sperm and enduring the long journey upstream. It is an amazing sight to watch these powerful swimmers battle their way upriver, occasionally performing vertical leaps four times their own length or more as they propel themselves over a rapid.

It was the Columbia River salmon that provided Lewis and Clark with much-needed food on their westward trek. Lewis, eating his first salmon in present-day Idaho, consumed it "with a very good relish." In addition to its taste, the Pacific-slope fish convinced him that he and Clark had crossed the Continental Divide. When they reached the Columbia after a spawning run of the salmon, Clark noted in his journal that the "number of dead Salmon on the shores and floating in the river is incredible."

The spawning habits of the salmon are a zoological marvel. After wandering two or three years in the trackless ocean, the fish find their way back to the exact stream of their birth. This homing instinct was considered more legend than fact until fish biologists noted that salmon from particular streams had certain racial characteristics: Their scales, for example, carried markings that differed from those of the fish in the next stream. This could only occur, the biologists reasoned, if a clan of salmon reproduced time after time in the same place and if few newcomers joined them to dilute the clan trait.

To prove their point, scientists made distinctive fin markings on millions of fingerling salmon before they left their native streams. Then the researchers went to sea, netted some of the same fish hundreds of miles from their home waters, and tagged them. Months later many of these fish that bore the original markings as well as the ocean tags returned to their childhood streams, unerringly selecting the correct branch of a tributary. Now few doubt the salmon's homing instinct, which is based on the "taste" of their home stream.

Most chinook salmon enter fresh water in the spring, although some migrate in the summer. Other salmon that use the Columbia River head upstream at other times of the year: the coho, or silver, salmon in the fall, the sockeye, or blueback, salmon in June or July, and the dog, or chum, salmon in the fall.

As the mature chinooks approach fresh water they undergo a dramatic transformation. The gray back and silvery belly of the male turns to blackish blotched with a dull red. The tail becomes cherry red and the jaws distort and often grow teeth half an inch long. In both sexes a growth of spongy skin covers the scales, particularly on the back. By spawning time the males have turned almost completely red.

Even though fishways have been built around the dams on the Columbia River up to the Chief Joseph Dam well upstream in

Canada goose

north central Washington, only a fraction of the homeward-bound salmon now complete their reproductive mission.

At Bonneville Dam east of Portland, Oregon, you can watch the salmon through a viewing window as they endeavor to find their way upriver through an elaborate fish ladder. Peering through the window into the swirling green water, you see the silvery salmon shining under lights as they struggle upstream.

If the fish do succeed in swimming past the fish ladders, they still face the perils of fishermen and polluted waters as they labor up the Columbia and into the Snake and Salmon rivers and their tributaries.

The survivors may travel almost to the Continental Divide to their spawning grounds in the headwaters of the well-named Salmon River. Here, often in brooks no wider than the fish's length, the journey ends. The female swishes her tail and body to hollow out a nest, or redd, in the gravel bottom and lays from three to eleven thousand eggs, each about a quarter of an inch in diameter. The male immediately swims over the eggs and ejects his sperm. Water temperature must be no warmer than fifty-four degrees Fahrenheit; if it is, the fish will delay spawning until it cools. Exhausted by their weeks of effort and too weak even to fight the current any longer, the adult salmon drift downstream to die.

When they hatch, the silvery young fry and fingerlings linger in fresh water for one to two years, growing slowly on a diet of small crustaceans. When the young (now two to three inches long) head downstream, they too have to run the gauntlet of the dams. Water plummeting over the spillways releases excess nitrogen and other gases. For many of the fish this water with its diminished oxygen content proves fatal. Others are stunned by the drop over a spillway or are buffeted as they pass through the whirling turbine blades of the power-generating plants. Still others die of a change of pressure, the same "bends" that is sometimes suffered by human deep-sea divers. Altogether, conservationists estimate, one-third of the fingerlings never make it. But those that do reach the ocean have a high survival rate; they feast on the abundant marine life for three or four years until they too head for river mouths to continue the salmon life cycle.

Canada Goose

The Canada goose, the most widely distributed of America's geese, is a familiar sight along many western rivers as well as along rivers and lakes in other parts of the country. Although many geese migrate along flyways from Alaskan or Canadian breeding grounds to Mexico, some of them winter in the interior valleys in the Northwest.

We caught a glimpse of these heavy-bodied, powerful birds with black heads and grayish wings when we visited the spectacular Hells Canyon gorge, the deepest river gorge in North America. Hells Canyon is the most dramatic segment of the Snake River, a river that uncoils in two great curves from its source within Grand Teton National Park to Pasco, Oregon, where it adds its fast-moving waters to those of the Columbia. The river forms part of the border between Idaho and Oregon, which is where Hells Canyon lies. At its deepest point Hells Canyon drops 7,900 feet, ever narrowing from the craggy heights of the Seven Devils Mountains to the whitewater rapids and swirling eddies of the river. This magnificent canyon, whose life zones vary from alpine growth at the rim to an arid floor, is deeper than the Grand Canyon by two thousand feet.

In the heart of the canyon, at Pittsburg Landing, Roy Lombardo, a seasonal ranger of the U. S. Forest Service, works to preserve the Hells Canyon National Recreation Area as a wild and scenic river. On a sunny April day Roy took us upriver in an aluminum jet boat.

The scenery was spectacular. Steep slopes of black basalt rock stairstepped up from the river on both sides as the mountain flanks shouldered their way toward the tree-clad rims. The sharp outlines of the rocks were softened by clumps of dark green shrubs and the light green of spring growth of cheat grass and bunchgrass. The vegetation finds what nourishment it can from the gritty soil, the residue of years of erosion of the rock and windblown dust. Terraced bluffs soared skyward in tiers of several hundred feet each. As towering as they seemed, they were only small steps in the sheer height of the canyon. So deep is this fissure in the earth that in only a few places can you actually see the rim from the river.

The noise of the boat flushed two Canada geese along the riverbank into the air with a flurry of wings. The two boldly patterned, heavy-bodied birds, one male and one female, flapped away up the river, honking loudly. Canada geese, Roy reminded us, are very attentive parents, especially in the springtime when they raise their young. "This pair, for example, may be flying upstream on purpose to draw attention away from their chicks," he said.

Their nest, a heap of grass or sticks, is usually tucked beneath a ledge in the cliffs where it is safely above any flooding and hidden from predators. There the mother goose incubates five or six creamy colored eggs for twenty-eight to thirty days until they hatch. Meanwhile, the male alternates between standing by to protect the nest and seeking food for the female and their offspring.

Within forty-eight hours of hatching, the greenish yellow goslings follow their father to the water, the mother bringing up the rear. The babies double their weight in a week but cannot fly—or escape from predators—for several weeks until they grow their wing feathers.

Another interesting parental action of the Canada goose, Roy added, is that the mother practically pushes the young out of the nest after they grow their feathers. She seems to sense that the goslings are safer in the water than they are on the nest where they are vulnerable to the hawks that sweep along the cliff face.

The chicks grow up to follow the same regular patterns as their parents. Around sunrise and again before sunset, Canada geese scatter to graze. Along the river they may dip underwater to nibble the roots of aquatic plants or fly farther afield to look for shoots of new crops. Between feedings they rest on the open water or on a nearby sandbar.

Mountain Lion

We glanced up a side canyon and spotted five mule deer nibbling on low browse. Mule deer are a common sight in the shrubby bottoms as well as on open slopes that occasionally break up the steep terrain. The prevalence of mule deer is undoubtedly one factor in the existence of a number of mountain lions, or cougars, in Hells Canyon.

In this wild country the mountain lion has the conditions it needs to survive: isolated stretches of wilderness unbroken by any but a few primitive roads and a plentiful supply of game such as deer, elk, and rabbits.

The mountain lion has a long, low torso and large padded feet that allow it to slip through tree cover or scrub country without a sound. Since its forelimbs are heavier and shorter than its hind legs, the animal walks with its hindquarters held higher than the rest of its body—the sign of a fast runner.

The big cat is capable of incredible physical feats such as leaping eighteen feet into a tree. When racing over rough terrain, the mountain lion moves smoothly and swiftly, balancing itself by swinging its long, heavy tail from side to side. Its great maneuverability and rapid acceleration enable the big cat to run down a deer before the prey can attain its top speed.

Hunting mostly at night, the mountain lion often travels long distances in search of its quarry. When stalking its prey, it brings it to the ground by leaping upon its back and seizing it by the neck. Or it may lie quietly along a branch to await its meal. Preying on weak, sickly, or older animals, the lion effectively thins out a herd of deer or elk. It is a master of staying out of sight, using cover such as rocks, thickets, or trees within its range. It maintains no permanent den. Rangers report that they occasionally see cougar tracks in the winter snow, but sighting the animal itself at any time of the year is rare.

Chukar Partridge

The valley supports a wide variety of other wildlife, including black bears, coyotes, lynxes, skunks, raccoons, chipmunks, marmots, grouse, and chukar partridges.

The chukar is a ground-dwelling bird that is brownish gray on its upper parts with a distinctive black-and-white striped pattern on its flanks. Other distinguishing characteristics are its red legs and the black "necklace" around its throat. It thrives in the canyon despite the meager cover of sagebrush and grass. The female often makes its nest under a sagebrush. The nest is a shallow depression scratched in the ground and lined with dry grass, stems, and feathers.

Chukars feed on a wide variety of plant species and relish green grass leaves, seeds, and forbs as well as the nuts of the piñon pine. Chukars are vulnerable to coyotes, great horned owls, golden eagles, and hawks for whom they are prey. When startled, the chukar breaks into a fast trot, preferring to dodge around boulders and bushes rather than take to the air. When trying to escape on foot, the chukar invariably runs uphill, dodging around rocks and boulders to outdistance its foe.

Marmot

The marmot lives not on the open slope like the chukar but in the nooks and crannies of rocky areas. The yellow-bellied marmot common in these parts is brown with a yellowish tinge to its coat and has a distinctive white splotch on its head between the eyes.

This western cousin of the eastern woodchuck chooses to make its home in the rocks to avoid predators such as bears, coyotes, golden eagles, and hawks. If you are in a rocky western canyon, listen for the high-pitched warning squeak it emits to warn other marmots of the approach of an intruder.

The marmot is about half the size of a woodchuck and weighs from eight to fifteen pounds. It fattens up all summer on a diet of lichens, roots, berries, and grasses, sometimes growing so fat that its belly drags on the ground. The extra weight serves it well when it goes into its long hibernation period during the winter. You might catch sight of one on a sunny day stretched out on a rock, resting and recuperating from a big meal, or barking to warn intruding visitors away from its territory.

Steelhead

The variety of wildlife, Roy told us, drew prehistoric people and later the Nez Perce Indians to the Snake River valley. Petroglyphs and pictographs that these ancient people inscribed on the rocks are found throughout the canyon; some of them depict hunting parties and portray the animals you still find in the canyon today.

The gorge, he said, probably attracted the Indians because winter temperatures here are surprisingly mild compared to temperatures on the high plateau. Even when snowstorms rage around the peaks at the canyon rim, little snow falls in the canyon itself. Temperatures at river level are often twenty to thirty degrees higher than those on more exposed terrain.

Fish were another resource that drew the Indians to the river. Bass, perch, crappie, and carp swim here today. But few of the flashing chinook that were once a major item in the Indian diet still make their way into Hells Canyon. Instead, on their run upriver from the ocean they leave the Snake River and turn into the Salmon River to spawn. The construction of the Hells Canyon Dam on the Snake River—a dam that has no fish ladders—cut off the chinook from their spawning grounds upriver on the Snake.

But if the chinook are missing, two other fish still put a gleam in the eye of the Snake River fisherman: the steelhead and the sturgeon. The steelhead is an anadromous fish that until recently was classified as a trout. But it has been reclassified as a salmon, according to fish biologists, because its anatomy, behavior, and internal molecular structure are more similar to other members of the salmon family.

Like other salmon, the steelhead migrates several hundred miles into the open ocean where it lives for several years before returning to fresh water once again to spawn. Some steelhead, raised in rivers of the Northwest, have been caught as far away as Japan.

When the steelhead leaves the ocean in the spring to begin its homeward journey, it is a brilliant silver. As it enters its home river and adapts once more to fresh water, it develops colors typical of the freshwater rainbow trout: dark greenish blue on its back, a crimson lateral band along its side, and black spots over most of its body. Steelhead spawn in the fall and their eggs hatch when water temperatures rise the following spring.

Sturgeon

The other remarkable fish found in the Snake River is the white sturgeon, a bottom-feeding fish that can reach an amazing size. The largest of America's freshwater fish, sturgeon average some sixty pounds in weight. The record size caught in U. S. rivers was

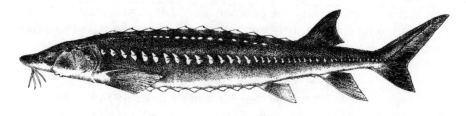

sturgeon

a 1,285-pound white sturgeon, twelve and one-half feet long, that was hooked in the Columbia River.

The sturgeon is a relic of prehistory; its direct forebears swam in the seas some 300 million years ago, as proved by fossilized remains that have been discovered. Today the sturgeon is found in only a few rivers in the country.

Most sturgeon mature for as long as twenty years in the ocean or in brackish water before they migrate up a river to spawn. The sturgeon that live in the Snake River, however, spend their entire lives in the river rather than migrating to the ocean.

This large fish is whitish or light gray in color and looks fiercer than it is. Five lateral rows of bony plates that lie along its back embedded in the skin make the fish look something like a seagoing dinosaur. Unlike most fish, it has no interior bony skeleton. The sturgeon has a half-moon-shaped mouth; a toothless tube protrudes downwards to suck in snails, clams, small fish, and insect larvae that may be liberally mixed with mud. Whisker-like appendages called chin barbels can feel a morsel before the fish gobbles it up.

The sturgeon is the champion egg producer among freshwater fishes. A single female may deposit two to three million eggs at one time. A female sturgeon full of eggs may add as much as 25 percent to her weight.

Trees

At the historic Kirkwood Ranch in upper Hells Canyon, visitors can glimpse what life was like on a canyon sheep ranch. In the early twentieth century some hundred families lived on ranches along the Snake River. Volunteer interpreter Violet Shirley, who grew up on one of these ranches, recounted what it was like.

Trees were important, she told us, and the ranchers welcomed almost any kind of tree for the shade it could provide against the searing summer sun and the heat at the canyon bottom. Summer temperatures average 106 degrees Fahrenheit, sometimes reaching 115 degrees.

A common tree in these parts, Violet continued, is the hackberry, a tree that grows to about fifteen feet in height and has rough, gnarled bark and a heart-shaped leaf. It thrives in the hot, dry climate, often growing near a watercourse where it sends down deep roots to tap the water below. She showed us one growing not far from the ranch house door.

Another tree that grows in Hells Canyon is a surprise—at least it was to a visiting botanist who told Violet she was mystified to find this tree outside the southeastern United States. This is the river birch, or red birch. Look for the serrated edges of its typical birch leaf and a whitish bark that separates from the trunk and peels back in places as the tree grows, showing the light pinkish brown tint of the freshly exposed layer beneath. No one knows how it got to Hells Canyon, but this tree that grows to eighty feet in height has found its natural habitat—along a watercourse.

Alders mix with cottonwoods and ash trees along tributary creeks, their grayish white bark similar to that of the aspen or beech. Another distinctive riparian plant is the matrimony bush, whose weeping branches bend to the ground then take root, enabling the bush to spread. The bush also bears thorns. The plant is so named, according to canyon lore, because like a marriage it possesses some thorns but with tender loving care it can survive.

Spotted Skunk

The ranchers may have welcomed trees on their property but they did not welcome visits from one of the most common animals in the canyon, the spotted skunk. Unlike most mammals that take advantage of protective coloration to camouflage themselves, skunks brazenly advertise their presence. They know they are well protected by the noxious odor they can eject from the scent glands they carry near the base of their tail.

Skunks are so numerous, Violet related, that during one summer she spent at Kirkwood Ranch she counted twenty-nine of them. Although the skunk is normally nocturnal, she said she saw them wandering around at all times of day. One night, she recalled, she was awakened by a noise in the kitchen of the ranchhouse. Investigating with a flashlight, she caught sight of a skunk sniffing around for food on the kitchen counter. Startled, it disappeared out the open kitchen window and went to look for its meal elsewhere.

Of all the skunks the spotted skunk is the most unmistakable with its series of broken white stripes decorating the neck, back, and sides. It also carries a white spot on the forehead and another under each ear. It is the smallest of the skunks, averaging only nine or thirteen inches long, not counting a tail half again as long as its body. With its pointed snout, rounded ears, and dark eyes hidden against its black fur, the skunk has an alert expression. Its glistening fur is dense and long, especially the white tail hairs. On each foot are five toes, each ending in sharp, curving claws that are longer on the front feet.

The skunk uses its sharp teeth to chop its food into small pieces. It is capable of making a variety of noises—usually grunts and screeches—and apparently is playful at games such as chasing crickets.

For its den the skunk seeks a rocky crevice, the deserted burrow of another animal, a brush pile, or a tree hollow. It may also find that the space beneath a ranch building is just the right place to raise its family. Several female skunks may den together in the winter, but the males tend to be solitary.

The spotted skunk compensates a rancher for its denning space by preying on mice and insects such as beetles and grasshoppers. Skunks also feed on berries, eggs, and any human handouts they can find. One day at a picnic Violet watched as a fearless skunk trotted up to a table where food was being served, stood on its hind legs beside a guest, and even tried to grab its share of the people food.

Peregrine Falcon

We rode out of Hells Canyon with two young biologists, Ed Levine and Matt Erickson, who were under contract with the Idaho Department of Fish and Game. They had been camping for three days in the canyon's backcountry searching for sites where they could safety release peregrine falcons to the wild. Soon they would return to Hells Canyon with several immature peregrine falcons bred under the auspices of the Peregrine Fund, a nonprofit conservation organization that seeks to restore the peregrine and other birds of prey to wilderness areas.

The Peregrine Fund's specialists breed raptors in captivity in such a way that the birds can still adapt to living in the wild. Through its efforts the Fund has successfully implanted some three thousand falcons in twenty-eight states where falcon populations had been greatly reduced in recent years by the harmful effects of the herbicide DDT. In 1975, according to the Fund, no peregrine falcons were left in the east and only twenty-seven pairs in the rest of the country; now three hundred pairs exist in the wild. With this success the organization is turning its attention to breeding other endangered raptors and releasing them in different parts of the world.

The peregrine, like other falcons, is smaller and more streamlined than other raptors and often chooses as its habitat a river like the Snake where it preys on ducks and other birds. Mostly slate-colored or blue-gray, its plumage fits tightly to its body; together with its long pointed wings this adapts it for speedy flight as it dive-bombs its victim. Like other raptors, the peregrine has large, powerful feet to grasp its prey.

To gradually accustom their young peregrines to being on their own in the wild, Ed and Matt said they would bring the raptors to the locations they had just selected, locations where prey and nesting materials are readily available to the birds and that are free of the falcon's own predators like the great horned owl. Ed and Matt, acting somewhat like surrogate parents, would place the falcons in a hacking box, or temporary home, and provide them with fresh-killed prey for about two weeks, introducing the food into the box secretly so the birds would be unaware of the human intervention. Gradually, Ed and Matt would reduce the food provided. As the falcons began to hunt on their own, the hacking box would be withdrawn, leaving the young peregrines to develop the inherent skills that make them one of the fastest diving raptors in the wild.

Great Horned Owl

As we jounced up the road beside a high cliff Ed suddenly brought the vehicle to a stop, motioning toward a white, blotchy streak on the rock wall. "Great horned owl on a nest," he said, pointing out the nest and the bird "whitewash" that painted the rock wall. "I'm glad this owl nest isn't near one of the hacking sites we just picked out," he confided.

We all climbed out and quietly moved closer, binoculars ready. Into our focus came a female great horned owl with the typical white ruff around its neck and two tufts sticking up that cover the bird's keen ears. It stood about two feet in height and its wings would have spanned five feet had they been extended. The mother owl sat on a nest of sticks that was held in place behind a small tree trunk that grew out of the cliff. She peered directly at us with her yellow-rimmed eyes, watching suspiciously as a young owlet fidgeted beneath her in the nest.

"With a nesting owl like this, it's important not to move so close the owl might think you are a threat," Ed said. "Some owls can be very aggressive when protecting their young and might even attack you."

The object of our attention was closely watching and listening to our movements below her. A great horned owl's eyes are ten times more sensitive than the human eye and cover a 60- to 70-degree field of vision. Like most owls, it has more rods in its eyes than you or I and thus can see objects better in the dark.

In addition to its excellent night vision, the great horned owl possesses something akin to stereo hearing. In one ear the inner ear opens into the lower chamber, while the opposite ear has its opening in the upper chamber, thereby permitting the owl to "triangulate" an incoming sound and get a fix on its prey even though it is unable to see it. The fluffy feathers that cover the ear openings filter the sounds for sharper hearing.

The owl's large wing area in comparison to its body weight permits it a slow wing beat that translates into quiet flight. Soft, fringed wing feathers further muffle the sound as it swoops in to seize a jackrabbit, bird, fish, scorpion, or skunk.

All at once a bush protruding from the cliff several feet below the nest shook. A young owl, wings half extended, flopped out onto a ledge, groping to hold itself against the cliff face.

"This must be baby brother," Ed laughed. "It's undoubtedly one of its first ventures out of the nest and it's learning its way around. It's probably saying to itself: 'What do I do now?'

"If it is stuck, the mother owl may bring it some food, but she won't come to its rescue because she knows how important it is for the youngster to learn to fly and thus be able to save itself from predators."

As we left the scene the young owl was still clinging to the rocks. Its mother peered over the edge of the nest at the flapping youngster, fulfilling its parental role of allowing its offspring to make its own mistakes and grow up by itself.

Prairie Falcon

A mottled brown-and-white prairie falcon with a three-foot wingspan glides from its nest in the cliff along the Snake River. Wings flapping, it circles higher and higher on an updraft. At an

Prairie falcon

appropriate altitude it swerves from the canyon to sweep inland over the sagebrush-covered rangeland. Then, suddenly folding its pointed wings, the falcon hurtles at a speed of about one hundred miles per hour toward the earth. From hundreds of feet above the ground the falcon has spotted a ground squirrel among the sage. Emitting a shrill cry, it dives to the earth's surface, pulling up at the last second as it grasps its prey in its powerful talons, killing it instantly.

The power dive of the prairie falcon and the actions of other raptors—golden eagles, hawks, and owls—are dramatically visible, perhaps better than anywhere else in North America, along an eighty-one-mile stretch of the lower Snake River in southwestern Idaho west of Boise. Here, where the river has cut high cliffs in the dark basalt rock, countless birds of prey find an environment that seems to perfectly fit their requirements.

The cliffs tower up to seven hundred feet above the river and provide ledges, crevices, and pinnacles that afford nesting places for these birds of prey, collectively known as raptors. Winds that blow against the canyon walls create updrafts that the birds ride to rise out of the canyon and hunt in the arid rangelands beyond the rim.

The adjacent land is covered with finely textured soil, much of it the result of ash from the eruption of Mount Mazama seven thousand years ago. This loose soil, called *loess*, seasonally teems with the Townsend ground squirrel, other rodents, and snakes that find it easy to burrow in the soft soil. Sagebrush and a low, blue-green bush called winterfat dot the flat landscape and serve as cover for the ground squirrels and for large numbers of jackrabbits, cottontail rabbits, ring-necked pheasants, mice, marmots, and rats. The winterfat also plays a role as an important food source for the ground squirrels, which are the top item on the menu of the area's extraordinary prairie falcon population, as well as of predatory land animals like the badger.

To help us understand how these various elements of an environmental mosaic fit together to provide a prime area for raptors, we took a driving tour with Karen Steenhof, associate research leader on the staff of the Birds of Prey Area, a 482,000-acre preserve along the river that is administered by the Bureau of Land Management. Each year an average of more than seven hundred pairs of raptors come to these cliffs along the Snake River to nest and raise their young. Other raptors, including the endangered bald eagle and the peregrine falcon, inhabit this riverside setting during their migration and wintering periods. At the Snake River Birds of Prey Area, Karen told us, hunting of raptors is prohibited, as it is all over the country. Another major threat to raptors in other areas—the effect of pesticides passed up through the food chain that reduces the thickness of their fragile eggs—has not been a problem in the wide open spaces at Birds of Prey. What's more, she added, the food chain of the prairie falcon and the golden eagle, two prime residents of the natural area, are short ones whereas the food chain of the bald eagle that was so severely affected by pesticides is a long one.

At one point we got out and walked to an overlook where you get a panoramic view of the Snake River far below and the palisaded cliffs along both sides.

"Don't be disappointed if you don't see a prairie falcon or a golden eagle right away," she warned us. We soon discovered why. You find yourself gazing at a sweep of a canyon that is five miles long and a mile wide. In that expanse you are hoping to catch sight of a bird that not only blends in with its surroundings but makes its home in a hidden cranny in the cliffs. Even when one of the big birds is airborne, it is only a solitary speck in the sky.

Suddenly Karen looked up to see, high in the sky above the canyon rim, a prairie falcon, the most common of the raptors at Birds of Prey. About 5 percent of the prairie falcons in the United States live on this preserve. To recognize a bird this high in the sky it helps to know its flight characteristics, which differ with each raptor. When the prairie falcon flies, for example, it flaps its wings rapidly several times, then glides, then flaps again.

We could barely hear the high-pitched call it gave to alert its mate that it was returning from a successful hunt over the tableland.

To be an effective hunter, the prairie falcon needs a lot of countryside for a territory. It uses a contour-hugging technique and flies low over the arid plain, capitalizing on its ability to surprise its prey rather than relying on superior eyesight as does the golden eagle.

Biologists who have studied the birds have found an interesting correlation between the falcons and the ground squirrels, their main prey. In January the ground squirrels emerge from a six-month estivation, or dormancy, to mate and have their young. At the same time, the prairie falcons arrive in the area from their winter home in Mexico and lay their eggs, which hatch eight to ten weeks later.

By the time the young prairie falcons have hatched, the baby ground squirrels have grown into juveniles and emerge from their burrows to feed on surface vegetation, thus providing excellent hunting for the adult falcons who have babies to feed. By July, when the ground squirrels go underground once more for their long dormancy period, the young falcons, all well fed, have fledged and the prairie falcon families leave the canyon to seek other hunting grounds.

Kestrel

Another airborne shape caught our eye. "An American kestrel," Karen identified as the bird flew low over our heads. The kestrel, or sparrow hawk, is the smallest of the falcon family, only a little larger than a robin. Brightly colored, it sports reddish, blue, and cinnamon feathers.

Perching on a treetop, its long tail flicking up and down, this bold and aggressive little falcon can drop like a flash on a small mammal such as a ground squirrel or lizard. Like other falcons it often uses certain favorite hunting perches that it occupies at regular intervals. The kestrel also possesses another talent that helps it hunt: it can hover in midair as its sharp eyes sweep the ground below for a grasshopper, mouse, or a vole. It brings captured prey back to the home it makes in a tree cavity, sometimes the abandoned home of a flicker or woodpecker.

Raven

We focused our binoculars on several ravens as they glided on motionless wings along a cliff face. The raven, all black, looks much like a crow but is twice the crow's size. In flight the raven flaps less and soars more than a crow. Using its fan-shaped tail as a rudder, it can circle for hours in a flat, eaglelike glide and ride the wind, hovering and sidestepping adeptly. Ravens even dive to earth like falcons or tumble in a series of somersaults.

Although not a raptor, the raven often makes its home with raptors like peregrine falcons, constructing its nest on a sheltered ledge over a sheer drop. The two species tolerate each other. Ravens often range in pairs and seem to mate for life, returning to the same cliff for many years. The raven builds a bulky nest of sticks lined with fur or other soft material. It subsists on a diet of insects, reptiles, and mice in addition to bird eggs and food morsels it steals from other birds. Many people feel the raven is a symbol of wilderness: the bird has retreated from developed areas but you still see numerous ravens in great open expanses like the Birds of Prey area.

Magpie

A magpie, another songbird, swooped in to perch on one of the interpretive signs, its white wing patches on a black body making it easy to spot. The magpie is one of the few birds with a tail longer than its body. Its scalloped wings—short and rounded—propel it aloft but do not qualify it as a rapid flier. The long wedge-shaped tail seems to get in the way when it tries to fly in a strong wind. On the ground it walks with short, jerky steps.

The magpie needs plenty of open rangeland as it forages for grasshoppers, rodents, and weevils. Magpies mate for life and build a unique type of nest, often within a stand of thick brush. Fashioning a mud cup, the birds line it with rootlets and surround it with a wall of sticks. Finally, they cover it with a dome of twigs to discourage marauders like hawks from discovering it.

Harrier

Leaving our high vantage point, we drove down into the canyon bottom. Far beneath the canyon rim in a marshy area along the riverbank we saw a pair of birds, one gray, the other brown, swooping over the wetland.

"Harriers," Karen said. "The male is mostly gray and has a white breast. The female is brown with a buff-colored breast. They're also called marsh hawks."

A medium-sized hawk, the harrier has a three-and-a-half-foot wingspan. Its keen sight and hearing help the harrier snag mice, ground squirrels, kangaroo rats, and voles, even when these rodents are hidden deep in the cattails and bulrushes of the marsh. To help it pick up the squeak of its prey in the high grass, it has facial discs around its eyes as owls do; these specialized feathers direct the sounds to its ears. The harrier is the only diurnal raptor (one that is active by day) to have such discs.

Harriers build their nests on the ground within the high vegetation; these nests may be a foot or more in diameter. The female lays her eggs between mid-April and mid-May, usually from three to nine in a clutch. After the chicks hatch, the male goes hunting for frogs, insects, fish, and small birds, then flies back to the nest to drop the prey to the nesting female. She sometimes catches his offerings in midair, then feeds them to their offspring.

Harriers are also known for their spectacular aerobatic flight patterns called sky dancing, a series of loops, rolls, and undulating flight patterns performed by the male as a courtship ritual.

harrier

Cliff Swallow

Karen guided the vehicle along a backcountry road that was more suited to a mule than a vehicle. As we approached two large potholes in the tire tracks ahead she braked to a stop as a cloud of small, dark brown birds swirled about and landed in the puddles of muddy water.

"These aren't raptors, of course," she smiled. "They're cliff swallows. A deep river canyon like this is a perfect habitat for them."

As we watched, one bird after another seemed to play follow the leader, landing at the edge of the puddle, plucking up a beakful of mud, then taking off immediately to head for the sheer cliffs that formed a backdrop for the river. Our binoculars told us the rest of the story. Each swallow flew with its small load of mud

golden eagle

to a miniature colony of tiny tan apartments clustered in an alcove in the cliff. At its home each bird added its contribution to the rounded adobe nests before returning for the next load.

Before a nesting pair of swallows completes the roof on their mud apartment, the female lays her four to five brown-spotted white eggs in the enclosure. Then the male proceeds to put on the roof, protecting the female and the eggs. A swallow colony often raises its young in the same nests year after year until the apartment complex finally falls apart.

Cliff swallows wheel and crisscross in flocks, snagging beetles and other insects from the air. They glide in long elliptical patterns, following each glide with a steep climb like a roller coaster. They congregate at dawn assemblies, squeaking guttural greetings to one another. In August and September, before cold weather drives away their insect food, the cliff swallows start toward South America, following one of the longest migration routes of American land birds.

Golden Eagle

The biggest thrill of our bumpy ride through the canyon came when we caught our first glimpse of a golden eagle, the largest raptor that nests at Birds of Prey.

Karen had set up her spotting scope on a tripod as she had done several times earlier, looking for a golden eagle nest that another staff member had reported. "There it is!" she announced. "I think there are two eaglets in the nest."

We took turns squinting through the scope. It brought into sharp focus a large nest of sticks built on a slab that jutted out from the steep rock face. Atop the nest perched the large brown bird. It was probably the mother eagle, which usually incubates the eggs and cares for the young, but it could have been the father because male and female golden eagles are difficult to tell apart. Every so often we saw two whitish-colored eaglets—just a couple of weeks old, Karen estimated—poke their heads above the rim.

The male eagle, she said, was probably close by watching the nest. If not, he would be flying the range hunting for food. When he returned, he would give his catch to the mother eagle who would bite it into pieces and feed it to her young.

Since this was a windy day, Karen pointed out, the mother eagle was probably staying at the nest not only to protect her off-spring from marauders but also to partially cover them with her broad wings to keep them warm.

The golden eagle gets its name from the golden-colored feathers on its head and upper neck. A good way to identify it is by the eagle's legs, which are feathered down to the toes. It takes about four years for an eagle to achieve its full dark plumage.

These majestic fliers have broad wings and rounded tails that enable them to soar effortlessly with their seven-foot wingspan for long periods of time. They flap their wings slowly and powerfully.

Their main food source in the Birds of Prey area is the black-tailed jackrabbit. One study done by the staff showed that the more jackrabbits roaming the tableland, the larger the number of eggs the female golden eagles lay. Since the eagles do not migrate but stay in Idaho throughout the year, they depend heavily on the jackrabbit population.

Each nesting pair of a species of golden eagles, Karen explained, stakes out its own territory based on the number of prey in that area and defends its hunting ground against competitors. As a result, she said, you will most likely find only one pair of golden eagles at any particular location in the canyon.

LAKES

In the mountainous West lakes form in pockets between the steep slopes, depressions formed by volcanic upheavals that long ago shaped much of the terrain in this part of the country. These mountain lakes are fed by rainfall and by runoff from the snows that drape the tops of some peaks all year long. On some mountains the snow piles up into snowfields and hardens into glaciers, which gradually melt and add their runoff to the lakes below.

The alpine glaciers have deepened the valleys and steepened their walls, creating cliffs and waterfalls, cirques, and lakes. Lake Chelan in North Cascades National Park in Washington, for example, lies in a glacially carved trough so deep that its bottom is about four hundred feet below sea level. A species of cod, the burbot, has adapted to live in this cold, deep water. The burbot is the only one of twenty-three species of North American cod and hake known to live in fresh water.

Other lakes result from precipitation that collects in open calderas of the volcanic peaks that typify the Pacific Mountain Range. The deepest of these is Crater Lake, the centerpiece of Crater Lake National Park in southern Oregon. Crater Lake fills the caldera of a now-extinct volcano known as Mount Mazama, a volcano that erupted with great force about seven thousand years ago. The explosions, geologists estimate, were forty-two times more powerful than the explosions that shook nearby Mount St. Helens in 1980. As the volcanic activity subsided, water began to collect in the bowl. Springs, snowfall, and rainfall filled it further, creating a lake 1,932 feet deep, the deepest in the United States. The volcano beneath has not stirred in a thousand years.

High mountain lakes like Crater Lake have an interesting characteristic that is readily apparent to the visitor: They are a much deeper blue or blue-green color than the lakes you see in other parts of the country. This brilliant color is due to the purity of the water and to a lack of algae. The growth of algae, which would lead to the growth of other plants and marine life, depends on the availability of various mineral elements including calcium, silicon, and potassium. These minerals often leach into the water from the soil and rocks underlying a drainage area. But where the terrain is dominated by granite or other hard rocks that are relatively insoluble, the amount of nutrients eroded by water runoff will be scant. As a result, the lake will be comparatively growth-free and the water will be clear. Like a daytime sky, these clear waters reflect blue and violet wavelengths strongly but absorb other colors or transmit them downward.

Many a mountain lake is rich in dissolved oxygen from the water that trickles in but poor in nitrogen, phosphorus, and the other minerals that would enable it to support plant and animal life. The familiar reeds and cattails you see growing on the fringes of other lakes do not grow in these clear mountain lakes.

But if little life exists in these high lakes, a variety of animals usually roam nearby. Forests of Douglas fir and western hemlock grow close to the edge of many lakes, providing good cover. Clearings and meadows full of plants and grasses supply plentiful forage for the numerous animals that make use of a lake as their water source.

Elk

The elk, the second largest member of the deer family after the moose, is a good swimmer and can swim across a lake if it needs to. But during the summer when they migrate to the mountain slopes, elks are more likely to be found in mountain meadows or forested uplands where they graze on grasses, sedges, broad-leafed herbs, and wild mushrooms.

Elks are both grazers and browsers. After grazing on grasses in the summer, they turn to browsing in the wintertime, eating twigs and needles of fir, juniper, and a variety of hardwood trees and shrubs. When the first snows come to the upper slopes, elks migrate down from the mountainsides to sheltered valleys and forests.

To get sufficient nutrients, an elk must consume a lot of forage. Like others in the deer family, the elk is a ruminant—it eats plant food that it chews and rechews. To efficiently digest its food, the animal has a four-chambered stomach. As the elk feeds, it swallows unchewed plant material, which goes into the first stomach chamber. While the animal rests or beds down after a feeding period it regurgitates mouthfuls of food and "chews its cud," or ruminates. The material is then reswallowed, eventually making its way to the last chamber, or the true stomach, where the contents are finally digested.

Strong, muscular animals, elks can run thirty miles an hour for short distances and can trot for miles at a time. Their senses of smell and hearing are both sharp. A bull elk stands about five feet high at the shoulder and weighs between seven hundred and one thousand pounds. Its coat is reddish brown in the summer; in winter it turns a tawny brown or brownish gray as course guard hairs grow to overlay its woolly underfur. Neck, chest, head, and underbelly are a darker brown, while the rump and tail have buff-colored or whitish hair.

Each year a bull grows large branching antlers that sweep upward and back from its head. Antlers begin to grow in late April or early May, growing through a stage of "velvet." Velvet is the soft covering of the growing antler that contains the blood vessels that supply nourishment to the antler. The antlers are fully grown by August. Then the elk rubs off the velvet that has dried up and is no longer needed. The animal loses its antlers in the late winter, preparatory to growing a new set the next year.

Cow elks have the same color coat as the males but grow no antlers. Cows often bark or grunt to communicate with their calves; the calves themselves make a squealing sound. The best-known elk call, however, is the bull's bugling, which he does primarily in mating season. It consists of a low bellow that ascends to a high note and continues until the animal runs out of breath, followed by guttural grunts. Cows also bugle at times.

During the mating season, in September and October, bulls bugle invitations to cows and challenges to other bulls. The males sometimes fight with each other, joining antlers and pushing and shoving. Battles rarely end in serious injury; the weaker bull usually breaks off the confrontation and trots away. Dominant bulls gather a harem of up to fifteen females along with their calves. The breeding season is long and takes its toll on the bull. He must use much energy to keep younger bulls from stealing his cows and to prevent the cows from wandering away.

Red Fox

Distributed widely across the United States—including the western states—the red fox patrols watery habitats such as lakes and rivers as well as open clearings, fields, and forests. Muskrats and frogs are among the variety of animals the fox preys upon. Other favorite prey of this opportunistic hunter are mice, rabbits, squirrels, opossums, birds, eggs, insects such as crickets and grasshoppers, and carrion, especially the carcasses of deer that have been killed by others.

The red fox, a member of the dog family, is a quick, agile hunter. You can identify it by its reddish brown coat and the bushy tail tipped with white. This large tail makes the fox seem larger than its average weight of eight to twelve pounds. It has distinctive pointed ears, a sharp snout, and thin muscular legs that suit it to run rapidly, trot for long distances, and pounce on its prey.

The fox has other attributes of a hunter as well: keen senses of sight, smell, and hearing (a fox can hear a mouse squeak a hundred feet away). A shy and cautious animal, it will often circle a possible food source several times, reconnoitering it, before approaching. It communicates and expresses its moods with a variety of sharp yaps, barks, howls, and screeches.

An intelligent animal, the fox will sometimes hide the remains of a kill in order to have food for a future occasion. During the mating season particularly, a dog fox (male) will cache its kill, digging a shallow hole in the ground or hiding its prize in a snowbank. When food runs short back at the den where the vixen is nursing the young, the male provider returns to its cache and carries the trophy back to its hungry mate.

Typically, the female fox gives birth in March or April to three to five cubs. The den may be located in a cavity dug into the bank of a river or lake, an unused woodchuck burrow, a hollow log, a brush pile, or a pile of rocks. Foxes usually make their dens close to water and may have several dens so they can move their young from place to place in case of danger.

As soon as the cubs are strong enough to be left alone for a time, the vixen returns to the hunt. When the cubs are about a month old, they too venture out of the den to lie in the sun or frolic about. By midsummer the young foxes start learning to hunt. At first they hunt in twos and threes, with one of the parents coaching from nearby. They sharpen their skills by catching a grasshopper or other small insect, then graduate to bigger game, and finally hunt alone. By early autumn the young males leave the home range to establish a territory of their own, perhaps traveling many miles before they find a suitable location not claimed by another fox. Young females may remain in their home territory if the food supply is plentiful; they may move on in late fall or early winter to find a better food supply and to locate a mate.

Moose

The large mammal that is best adapted to living in a watery habitat is the moose, the largest member of the deer family. The moose is easy to recognize by its large size (up to one thousand pounds), humped back, and dark reddish brown hide. Its coat fades to gray or grayish brown on the belly and lower parts of the legs.

The bull wears large palmlike antlers that spread six feet or more and grow during the spring and summer, then fall off in the winter as do the antlers of elk and deer. The cow moose grows no antlers. The moose has a long muzzle; the upper part hangs three or four inches over its chin. A *bell*, an unusual growth of skin covered with hair, hangs beneath its throat.

Despite its large size a moose can run up to thirty-five miles an hour. When it runs, it lifts each leg straight upward, a very different gait from other members of the deer family but particularly adapted to the moose's aquatic habitat. This leg action allows the animal to lift each leg easily out of a muddy lake or stream bottom. The moose also has large dewclaws (vestigial hooves) on the rear of each hind leg, which probably help keep the heavy animal from sinking too deeply into the muddy ooze.

Throughout the summer season moose visit lakes, rivers, streams, and ponds to rid themselves of flies and to feed on water plants. They are excellent swimmers and do not hesitate to cross a lake or river. They also like to roll in mud holes and eat the salty earth at salt licks. When it feeds in the water, the moose shows no fear of putting its head under. It relishes water lilies and will wade far out into a swampy pond or lake edge, munching plants on the surface or dipping its great head underwater to get at succulent roots. A moose can immerse its head in the water for a full minute as it eats the lake vegetation.

When not in the water, moose browse on the twigs and leaves of many kinds of plants and trees. Since they have no upper front teeth, they snap off twigs and pull off bark using the upper lip and lower incisors. Moose are big eaters, consuming an average of forty-five pounds a day of their strictly vegetarian diet.

Moose live alone during the summer, although a cow moose feeds along with her calf. They herd together more in the winter. Both males and females sometimes gather in small bands in swamps and woods where they find protection from the cold winds. Look for moose near rivers and lakes in the northern Rocky Mountains as well as in the northern tier of states bordering the Great Lakes and in northern New England. Hundreds of thousands of moose still roam many parts of Canada and Alaska.

It's Your Turn

The lakes and rivers of the Northwest brought an end to our travels to America's aquatic environments—just as they had provided the conclusion to the explorations of Meriwether Lewis and William Clark in an earlier day.

The explorers wrote in their journals of the many plants and animals they had observed, many of them never before seen by white men. The numerous species of wildlife and vegetation that Lewis and Clark described still exist along the shores of rivers and lakes today. In the national parks and national wildlife refuges, and along the national scenic rivers, are preserved a whole panorama of living things that thrive close to the water.

These wonders are waiting for you to experience at public preserves, and at rivers and lakes anywhere in the country. If you visit a river or lake park or refuge you will find, as we did, knowledgeable and enthusiastic rangers ready to help you get a better understanding and appreciation of this watery world of wildlife.

APPENDIX A

How to Rate a Rapid

Canoeists, kayakers, or rafters who plan to run a wild or scenic river judge the rapids ahead of them according to the International Scale of River Difficulty.

The difficulty of a rapid may vary with the water level: high water may cover up a stretch of rapids entirely but make other rapids more difficult. The following classifications apply to rapids at normal water levels.

Class I
Easy rapids with small waves and few obstructions.
Class II
Rapids with waves up to three feet high; some maneuvering is required.
Class III
Difficult rapids with high, irregular waves capable of swamping an open canoe; narrow chutes may require extensive maneuvering.
Class IV
Long, turbulent rapids with high, irregular waves, constricted passages, and blind drops; portages sometimes required.
Class V
Long, violent rapids with steep drops or waterfalls; hazardous in the event of a mishap; runnable only by experts.
Class VI
Class V difficulty carried to the extremes of navigability; great risk to life; runnable only by teams of experts with rescue skills and equipment.

(River runners on the Colorado River use a similar classification system for rapids but base it on ten instead of six as the highest degree of difficulty.)

U.S. Rivers and Lakes Preserved for Public Use

Rivers and lakes are national resources that contribute to the quality of our lives. Where are the best places to observe and enjoy these waterways in their natural state? More than 425 river and lake segments throughout the country are protected by law in one of three ways. They are listed below by state within three conservation categories:

A. River segments and lakes administered by the National Park Service (shown with administering national park and its designation).
B. Rivers designated under the Wild and Scenic Rivers Act as wild, scenic, and/or recreational and administered by other federal, state, or local agencies (agency shown in parenthesis).
C. State designated rivers (state river programs are identified by name and date of authorization, number of river miles protected, and names of designated rivers).

Other rivers and lakes not listed here are preserved within state parks, by other government agencies, and within private and corporate landholdings.

Alabama

A. None
B. Sipsey Fork of the West Fork River (National Forests in Alabama); Wild and Scenic
C. No established state river program

Alaska

A. Alagnak River (Katmai National Park and Preserve); Wild
Alatna River (Gates of the Arctic National Park and Preserve); Wild

Aniakchak River (Katmai
National Park and Preserve);
Wild
Charley River (Yukon-Charley
Rivers National Preserve);
Wild
Chilikadrotna River (Lake Clark
National Park and Preserve);
Wild
John River (Gates of the Arctic
National Park and Preserve);
Wild
Kobuk River (Gates of the
Arctic National Park and
Preserve); Wild
Lake Clark (Lake Clark National
Park and Preserve)
Mulchatna River (Lake Clark
National Park and Preserve);
Wild
Noatak River (Gates of the
Arctic National Park and
Preserve; Kobuk Valley
National Park); Wild
North Fork of the Koyukuk
River (Gates of the Arctic
National Park and Preserve);
Wild
Salmon River (Kobuk Valley
National Park); Wild
Tinayguk River (Gates of the
Arctic National Park and
Preserve); Wild
Tlikakila River (Lake Clark
National Park and Preserve);
Wild
B. Andreafsky River (U.S. Fish
and Wildlife Service); Wild
Beaver Creek (Bureau of Land
Management, Yukon Flats
National Wildlife Refuge); Wild

Birch Creek (Bureau of Land
Management); Wild
Delta River (Bureau of Land
Management); Wild, Scenic,
and Recreational
Fortymile River (Bureau of
Land Management); Wild,
Scenic, and Recreational
Gulkana River (Bureau of Land
Management); Wild
Ivishak River (U.S. Fish and
Wildlife Service); Wild
Nowitna River (U.S. Fish and
Wildlife Service); Wild
Selawik River (U.S. Fish and
Wildlife Service); Wild
Sheenjek River (U.S. Fish and
Wildlife Service); Wild
Unalakleet River (Bureau of
Land Management); Wild
Wind River (U.S. Fish and
Wildlife Service); Wild
C. Alaska Recreational Rivers
Program (1988); 544 river
miles protected
Alexander Creek
Kenai River Special
Management Area
Kroto Creek/Moose Creek
Lake Creek
Little Susitna River
Talachulitna River
Talkeetna River

Arizona
A. Colorado River (Grand
Canyon National Park)
B. Verde River (Prescott
National Forest); Wild and
Scenic

C. No established state river program

Arkansas

A. Buffalo National River
B. None
C. Arkansas Natural and Scenic River Commission (1979); no designated rivers; studying fourteen rivers

California

A. Kern River (Sequoia National Park, Sequoia National Forest); Wild, Scenic, and Recreational
Kings River (Kings Canyon National Park, Sequoia National Forest); Wild and Recreational
Merced River (Yosemite National Park, Sierra National Forest, Bureau of Land Management); Wild, Scenic, and Recreational
Tuolumne River (Yosemite National Park, Stanislaus National Forest, Bureau of Land Management); Wild, Scenic, and Recreational
B. American River, North Fork (Tahoe National Forest, Bureau of Land Management); Wild
American River, Lower (California Resources Agency); Recreational
Eel River (California Resources Agency, U.S. Forest Service, Bureau of Land Management, Round Valley Indian Reservation); Wild, Scenic, and Recreational
Feather River, Middle Fork (Plumas National Forest); Wild, Scenic, and Recreational
Klamath River (California Resources Agency, U.S. Forest Service, Bureau of Land Management, Hoopa Valley Indian Reservation, National Park Service); Wild, Scenic, and Recreational
Smith River (California Resources Agency, U.S. Forest Service); Wild, Scenic, and Recreational
Trinity River (California Resources Agency, Bureau of Land Management, U.S. Forest Service, Hoopa Valley Indian Reservation); Wild, Scenic, and Recreational
C. California Wild and Scenic Rivers System (1972); 1,325 river miles protected
East Carson River
Eel River System
Klamath River System
Lower American River
North Fork, American River
Smith River System
Trinity River System
West Walker River

Colorado

A. Gunnison River (Black Canyon of the Gunnison National Monument)
B. Cache de Poudre River (Arapaho and Roosevelt National Forests); Wild and Recreational
C. No established state river program

Connecticut

A. None
B. None
C. Connecticut River Protection Commission (1984); no rivers designated

Delaware

A. None
B. None
C. No established state river program

Florida

A. None
B. Loxahatchee River (Florida Department of Natural Resources); Wild, Scenic, and Recreational
C. Florida Scenic and Wild Rivers Program (1972 and 1978); 49 river miles protected
Loxahatchee River
Myakka River
Wekiva River

Georgia

A. Chattahoochee River (Chattahoochee River National Recreation Area)
B. Chattooga River (Chattahoochee National Forest); Wild, Scenic, and Recreational
C. Georgia Scenic Rivers Program (1969); 74 river miles protected
Chattooga River
Conasauga River
Ebenezer Creek
Jacks Fork

Hawaii

A. None
B. None
C. No established state river program

Idaho

A. None
B. Clearwater River, Middle Fork (Clearwater National Forest); Wild and Recreational
Rapid River (Hells Canyon National Recreation Area, U.S. Forest Service); Wild
Saint Joe River (Idaho Panhandle National Forest); Wild and Recreational
Salmon River (Salmon National Forest); Wild and Recreational

Salmon River, Middle Fork
  (Challis National Forest);
  Wild and Recreational
Snake River (Hells Canyon
  National Recreation Area,
  U.S. Forest Service); Wild
  and Scenic
C. Idaho Protected Rivers
  Program (1988); no rivers
  designated

Illinois
A. None
B. Vermilion River, Middle Fork
  (Illinois Department of
  Conservation); Scenic
C. No established state river
  program

Indiana
A. Indiana Dunes National
  Lakeshore
B. None
C. Indiana Natural and Scenic
  Rivers Program (1973 and
  1978); 107 river miles
  protected
Blue River
Cedar Creek
Wildcat Creek

Iowa
A. None
B. None
C. Iowa Protected Water Areas
  Program (1984); studying
  one river

Kansas
A. None
B. None
C. No established state river
  program

Kentucky
A. Cumberland River (Big
  South Fork National River
  and Recreation Areaa)
B. None
C. Kentucky Wild Rivers
  Program (1972); 110 river
  miles protected
Big South Fork, Cumberland
  River
Green River
Little South Fork, Cumberland
  River
Main Stem, Cumberland River
Martins Fork
North Fork, Red River
Rockcastle River
Rock Creek

Louisiana
A. None
B. Saline Bayou (Kisatchie
  National Forest); Scenic
C. Louisiana Natural and Scenic
  Streams System (1970); 1,250
  river miles protected
Amite River
Bashman Bayou
Bayou Bartholomew
Bayou Bienvenue
Bayou Chaperon
Bayou Cocodrie (Concordia)

Bayou Cocodrie (Evangeline)
Bayou D'Arbonne
Bayou Des Allemands
Bayou Dupre
Bayou Kisatchie
Bayou L'Outre
Bayou La Branche
Bayou Penchant
Bayou Sara
Bayou Trepangnier
Big Creek
Black Lake Bayou
Blind River
Bogue Chitto River
Bradley Slough
Calcasieu River
Chappepella Creek
Comite River
Dorcheat Bayou
Fish Creek
Holmes Bayou
Lake Borgne Canal
Little River
Middle Fork of Bayou
    D'Arbonne
Pirogue Bayou
Pushepatapa Creek
Saline Bayou (Bienville)
Saline Bayou (Catahoula)
Six Mile Creek
Spring Creek
Tangipahoa River
Tchefuncte River
Ten Mile Creek
Terre Beau Bayou
Tickfaw River
Trout Creek
West Pearl River
Whiskey Chitto Creek
Wilson Slough

Maine
A. None
B. Allagash Wilderness
    Waterway (State of Maine);
    Wild
C. Maine Rivers Policy (1982
    and 1983); about 1,500 river
    miles protected
Allagash River
Aroostook River
Dead River
Dennys River
East Branch, Penobscot River
East Machias River
Lower Kennebec River
Machias River
Main Stem, Penobscot River
Mattawamkeag River
Moose River
Narraguagus River
Rapid River
Saco River
Sheepscot River
St. John River
Upper West Branch, Penobscot
    River
West Branch, Penobscot River
West Branch, Pleasant River

Maryland
A. None
B. None
C. Maryland Scenic and Wild
    Rivers Program (1968, 1976,
    1977) 441 river miles
    protected
Anacostia River
Deer Creek
Monocacy River

Patuxent River
Pocomoke River
Potomac River
Severn River
Wicomico River
Youghiogheny River

Massachusetts

A. None
B. None
C. Massachusetts Scenic Rivers
   Program (1971 and 1977); 86
   river miles protected
Charles River
Mashpee River
Merrimack River
Money Brook/Hopper Brook
North River

Michigan

A. Pictured Rocks National
   Lakeshore
Sleeping Bear Dunes National
   Lakeshore
B. Au Sable River (Huron-
   Manistee National Forest);
   Scenic
Pere Marquette River (Huron-
   Manistee National Forest);
   Scenic
C. Michigan Natural Rivers
   Program (1971 and 1977);
   1,698 river miles protected
Au Sable River
Betsie River
Boardman River
Flat River
Fox River

Huron River
Jordan River
Kalamazoo River
Pere Marquette River
Pigeon River
Rifle River
Rogue River
Two Hearted River
White River

Minnesota

A. Lower Saint Croix National
   Scenic Riverway
Mississippi National River and
   Recreation Area
Saint Croix National Scenic
   Riverway
Voyageurs National Park
B. Lower Saint Croix Riverway
   (Minnesota Department of
   Natural Resources,
   Wisconsin Department of
   Natural Resources);
   Recreational
C. Minnesota Wild, Scenic, and
   Recreational Rivers Program
   (1973); 440 river miles
   protected
Cannon River
Kettle River
Minnesota River (Project
   Riverbend)
Minnesota River
Mississippi River (Headwaters
   Board)
Mississippi River
North Fork, Crow River
Rum River

Mississippi

A. None
B. Black Creek (DeSoto National Forest); Scenic
C. No established state river program

Missouri

A. Current River (Ozark National Scenic Riverways)
Jack Fork River (Ozark National Scenic Riverways)
B. Eleven Point River (Mark Twain National Forest); Scenic
C. No established state river program

Montana

A. None
B. Flathead River (Flathead National Forest, National Park Service); Wild, Scenic, and Recreational
Missouri River (Bureau of Land Management); Wild, Scenic, and Recreational
C. No established state river program

Nebraska

A. Missouri National Recreational River (Midwest Region, National Park Service); Recreational

B. None
C. No established state river program

Nevada

A. None
B. None
C. No established state river program

New Hampshire

A. None
B. Wildcat Creek (White Mountain National Forest, Town of Jackson), Scenic and Recreational
C. New Hampshire Rivers Management Protection Program (1988); 120 river miles protected
Lamprey River
Lower Merrimack River
Saco River
Swift River
Upper Merrimack River

New Jersey

A. Delaware National Scenic River (Delaware Water Gap National Recreation Area)
B. None
C. New Jersey Wild and Scenic River System (1977); 14 river miles protected
Atsion River

New Mexico

A. None
B. Rio Chama (Bureau of Land Management, Santa Fe National Forest); Wild and Scenic
   Rio Grande (Bureau of Land Management); Wild and Recreational
C. No established state river program

New York

A. Delaware National Scenic River (Delaware Water Gap National Recreation Area); Scenic
   Upper Delaware Scenic and Recreational River; Scenic and Recreational
B. None
C. New York Wild, Scenic, and Recreational Rivers System (1972); 1,248 river miles protected
   Rivers in Adirondack Park:
Ampersand Brook
Ausable River
Black River
Blue Mountain Stream
Bog River
Boreas River
Bouquet River
Cedar River
Cold River
Deer River
East Branch, Ausable River
East Branch, Sacandaga River
East Branch, St. Regis River
East Canada Creek
Hudson River
Independence River
Indian River
Jordan River
Kunjamuk River
Long Pond Outlet
Main Branch, Ausable River
Main Branch, Moose River
Main Branch, Oswegatchie River
Main Branch, Sacandaga River
Main Branch, Saranac River
Main Branch, St. Regis River
Marion River
Middle Branch, Grasse River
Middle Branch, Oswegatchie River
North Branch, Grasse River
Opalescent River
Otter Brook
Piseco Outlet
Raquette River
Red River
Rock River
Round Lake Outlet
Salmon River
Schroon River
South Branch, Grasse River
South Branch, Moose River
South Branch, West Canada Creek
West Branch, Ausable River
West Branch, Moose River
West Branch, Oswegatchie River
West Branch, Sacandaga River
West Branch, St. Regis River
West Canada Creek
West Stony Creek

Other New York Rivers:
Carmens River
Connetquot River
Nissequoge River
Ramapo River
Shawangank Kill

North Carolina

A. None
B. Horsepasture River
   (Nantahala National Forest);
   Scenic and Recreational
New River, South Fork (Stone
   Mountain State Park); Scenic
Chattooga River
   (Chattahoochee National
   Forest); Wild, Scenic, and
   Recreational
C. North Carolina Natural and
   Scenic Rivers System (1971);
   141 river miles protected
Linville River
Lumber River
South Fork, New River

North Dakota

A. None.
B. None.
C. No established state river
   program

Ohio

A. Cuyahoga River (Cuyahoga
   Valley National Recreation
   Area)
B. Little Beaver Creek (Ohio
   Department of Natural
   Resources); Scenic

Little Miami River (Ohio
   Department of Natural
   Resources); Scenic and
   Recreational
C. Ohio Scenic Rivers Program
   (1968 and 1972); 632 river
   miles protected
Big Darby Creek
Chagrin River
Grande River
Little Beaver Creek
Little Darby Creek
Little Miami River
Maumee River
Olentangy River
Sandusky River
Upper Cuyahoga River

Oklahoma

A. None
B. None
C. Oklahoma Scenic River
   Program (1977); 151 river
   miles protected
Big Lee's Creek
Flint Creek
Illinois River
Little Lee's Creek
Upper Mountain Fork River

Oregon

A. Crater Lake National Park
B. Big Marsh Creek (Deschutes
   National Forest);
   Recreational
Chetco River (Siskiyou
   National Forest); Wild,
   Scenic, and Recreational

Clackamas River (Mount Hood National Forest); Scenic, and Recreational

Crescent Creek (Deschutes National Forest); Recreational

Crooked River (Bureau of Land Management); Recreational

Crooked River, North Fork (Bureau of Land Management, Ochoco National Forest); Wild, Scenic, and Recreational

Deschutes River (Deschutes National Forest, Bureau of Land Management); Scenic and Recreational

Donner and Blitzen River (Bureau of Land Management); Wild

Eagle Creek (Wallowa-Whitman National Forest); Wild, Scenic, and Recreational

Elk River (Siskiyou National Forest); Wild and Recreational

Grande Ronde River (Bureau of Land Management, Umatilla National Forest, Wallowa-Whitman National Forest); Wild and Recreational

Illinois River (Siskiyou National Forest); Wild, Scenic, and Recreational

Imnaha River (Wallowa-Whitman National Forest); Wild, Scenic, and Recreational

John Day River (Bureau of Land Management); Recreational

John Day River, North Fork (Umatilla National Forest); Wild, Scenic, and Recreational

John Day River, South Fork (Bureau of Land Management); Recreational

Joseph Creek (Wallowa-Whitman National Forest); Wild

Little Deschutes River (Deschutes National Forest); Recreational

Lostine River (Wallowa-Whitman National Forest); Wild, and Recreational

Malheur River (Malheur National Forest); Scenic, and Recreational

Malheur River, North Fork (Malheur National Forest); Scenic

McKenzie River (Willamette National Forest); Recreational

Metolius River (Deschutes National Forest); Scenic, and Recreational

Minam River (Wallowa-Whitman National Forest); Wild

North Powder River (Wallowa-Whitman National Forest); Scenic

North Umpqua River (Umpqua National Forest, Bureau of Land Management); Recreational

Owyhee River (Bureau of Land Management); Wild

Owyhee River, North Fork

(Bureau of Land Management); Wild

Owyhee River, West Little (Bureau of Land Management); Wild

Powder River (Bureau of Land Management); Scenic

Quartzville Creek (Bureau of Land Management); Recreational

Rapid River (Hells Canyon National Recreation Area, U.S. Forest Service); Wild

Roaring River (Mount Hood National Forest); Wild and Recreational

Rogue River (Bureau of Land Management, Siskiyou National Forest); Wild, Scenic, and Recreational

Salmon River (Mount Hood National Forest, Bureau of Land Management); Wild, Scenic, and Recreational

Sandy River (Bureau of Land Management, U.S. Forest Service); Wild, Scenic, and Recreational

Smith River, North Fork (Siskiyou National Forest); Wild and Scenic

Snake River (Hells Canyon National Recreation Area, U.S. Forest Service); Wild and Scenic

Sprague River, North Fork (Fremont National Forest); Scenic

Squaw Creek (Deschutes National Forest); Wild and Scenic

Sycan River (Fremont National Forest, Winema National Forest); Scenic and Recreational

Upper Rogue River (Rogue River National Forest); Wild and Scenic

Wenaha River (Umatilla National Forest); Wild, Scenic, and Recreational

White River (Bureau of Land Management, Mount Hood National Forest); Scenic and Recreational

Willamette River, North Fork of Middle Fork (Willamette National Forest); Wild, Scenic, and Recreational

C. Oregon Scenic Waterways Program (1970 and 1988); about 1,100 river miles protected

Clackamus River

Deschutes River

Elk River

Grande Ronde River

Illinois River

John Day River

Klamath River

Little North Santiam River

McKenzie River

Metolius River

Minam River

Nestucca River

North Fork of Middle Fork of Willamette River

North Umpqua River

Owyhee River
Rogue River
Sandy River
Waldo Lake
Walker Creek
Wallowa River

Pennsylvania

A. Delaware National Scenic
   River (Delaware Water Gap
   National Recreation Area);
   Scenic
Delaware Water Gap National
   Recreation Area
Upper Delaware Scenic and
   Recreational River; Scenic
   and Recreational
B. None
C. Pennsylvania Scenic Rivers
   Program (1972); 393 river
   miles protected
Bear Run
French Creek
Lehigh River
LeTort Spring Run
Lick Run
Lower Brandywine River
Octoraro Creek
Schuylkill River
Stony Creek
Tucquan Creek

Rhode Island

A. None
B. None
C. No established state river
   program

South Carolina

A. Congaree Swamp National
   Monument
B. Chattooga River
   (Chattahoochee National
   Forest); Wild, Scenic, and
   Recreational
C. South Carolina Scenic Rivers
   Program (1974 and 1981); 5
   river miles protected
Middle Saluda River

South Dakota

A. Missouri National
   Recreational River (Midwest
   Region National Park
   Service); Recreational
B. None
C. South Dakota Wild, Scenic,
   and Recreational Rivers
   System (1972); No rivers
   designated

Tennessee

A. Obed Wild and Scenic River;
   Wild
Cumberland River (Big South
   Fork National River and
   Recreation Area)
B. None
C. Tennessee Scenic Rivers
   Program (1968); 318 river
   miles protected
Blackburn Fork River
Buffalo River
Conasauga River
French Broad River

Harpeth River
Hatchie River
Hiwassee River
Roaring River
Spring Creek
Tuckahoe Creek

Texas

A. Rio Grande Wild and Scenic
   River (Big Bend National
   Park); Wild and Scenic
B. None
C. No established state river
   program

Utah

A. None
B. None
C. No established state river
   program

Vermont

A. None
B. None
C. Vermont Comprehensive
   State Rivers Program (1987);
   No rivers designated

Virginia

A. None
B. None
C. Virginia Scenic Rivers
   System (1970); 169 river
   miles protected
Appomattox River

Catoctin Creek
Goose Creek
Hottoway River
James River
Rappahannock River
Rivanna River
Shenandoah River
St. Marys River
Staunton River

Washington

A. Lake Chelan National
   Recreation Area
Ross Lake National Recreation
   Area
B. Klickitat River (Gifford
   Pinchot National Forest);
   Recreational
Skagit River (Mount Baker-
   Snoqualmie National Forest);
   Scenic and Recreational
White Salmon River (Gifford
   Pinchot National Forest);
   Scenic
C. Washington Scenic Rivers
   Program (1977); 67 river
   miles protected
Beckler River
Green River
Main Stem, Skyomish River
North Fork, Skyomish River
South Fork, Skyomish River
Tye River

West Virginia

A. Bluestone National Scenic
   River (New River Gorge
   National River); Scenic

Gauley River National
  Recreation Area (New River
  Gorge National River)
New River Gorge National River
B. None
C. West Virginia Natural
  Streams Preservation System
  (1969); 236 river miles
  protected
Anthony Creek
Cranberry River
Greenbriar River
Meadow River
New River Gorge

Wisconsin

A. Apostle Islands National
  Lakeshore
Lower Saint Croix National
  Scenic Riverway
Saint Croix National Scenic
  Riverway
B. Lower Saint Croix Riverway
  (Wisconsin Department of
  Natural Resources;

Minnesota Department of
  Natural Resources);
  Recreational
Wolf River (Menominee Indian
  Tribe of Wisconsin, National
  Park Service); Scenic
C. Wisconsin Wild Rivers
  Program (1965); 327 river
  miles protected
Black River
Brule River
Flambeau River
Namekagon River
Pike River
Pine River
Popple River
St. Croix River
Wisconsin River
Wolf River

Wyoming

A. None
B. None
C. No established state river
  program

Index